The art of Persuasion

Learn the art of influencing, deception, mind games and hypnotism to Control the minds

Oliver Brain

© Copyright 2019 by Oliver Brain- All rights reserved.

This document is geared towards providing exact and reliable information in regards to the topic and issue covered. The publication is sold with the idea that the publisher is not required to render accounting, officially permitted, or otherwise, qualified services. If advice is necessary, legal or professional, a practiced individual in the profession should be ordered.

- From a Declaration of Principles which was accepted and approved equally by a Committee of the American Bar Association and a Committee of Publishers and Associations.

In no way is it legal to reproduce, duplicate, or transmit any part of this document in either electronic means or in printed format. Recording of this publication is strictly prohibited and any storage of this document is not allowed unless with written permission from the publisher. All rights reserved.

The information provided herein is stated to be truthful and consistent, in that any liability, in terms of inattention or otherwise, by any usage or abuse of any policies, processes, or directions contained within is the solitary and utter responsibility of the recipient reader. Under no circumstances will any legal responsibility or blame be held against the publisher for any reparation, damages, or monetary loss due to the information herein, either directly or indirectly.

Respective authors own all copyrights not held by the publisher.

The information herein is offered for informational purposes solely, and is universal as so. The presentation of the information is without contract or any type of guarantee assurance.

The trademarks that are used are without any consent, and the publication of the trademark is without permission or backing by the trademark owner. All trademarks and brands within this book are for clarifying purposes only and are the owned by the owners themselves, not affiliated with this document.

Contents

Chapter 1: What is persuasion

1.1 Introduction

Persuasion, the process by which actions or activities of an individual are, without restriction, affected by other people's communications. Other variables (for example, verbal threats, physical intimidation, one's physiological states) also influence one's attitudes and behaviors. Not all communication is meant to be persuasive; information or entertainment are other purposes. Sometimes, persuasion includes influencing individuals, and many consider the activity distasteful for this reason. Others might claim that the human community is disordered without some degree of social interaction and mutual compromise achieved by persuasion. In this way, by considering the alternatives, persuasion achieves social acceptability. To paraphrase Winston Churchill's evaluation of democracy as a form of government, persuasion is the worst form of social control except for all the others.

Persuasion. You may think of something positive or negative when you think of the word. Some people may think of peer pressure, like a person in authority telling you to do something, or else you're not going to fit in. Similarly, you might think of a salesman trying to get you to purchase his goods. Whatever comes to mind, for everyone to know, persuasion is an interesting concept. At some point, we're just trying to persuade someone and it's necessary to survive. We have to persuade somebody to be the best person for the job. We have to persuade somebody to reduce the price of what we want to buy. We're going to look at persuasion and its many dimensions in this chapter.

1.2 Persuasion affects everyone

You are re a smart person, so you know that nothing can change your mind. Nobody is going to advertise you openly or strive to get you to do something you don't want to do. And while you can often resist pushy people, persuasion is more than just someone trying to push on you their values or goods. In the shape of something more nuanced, persuasion may arrive, and you may be shocked at how much it can influence you. Persuasion can be either positive or negative. It's, in fact, negative. You can be tempted, on the one hand, to do alcohol. You can also be persuaded, however, to leave it too. You've been persuaded to do something in your career, no matter who you are. So, what's Persuasion? Persuasion can be broken down into a few small definitions, but it is a symbolic process that is the basic definition. That process makes people try to persuade others to carry habits or actions out and transform them into something we want them to be.

1.3 Factors of Persuasion

Persuasive factors include:

- it's symbolic
- It's trying to use every signal it can to persuade you, including images, noises, phrases, etc.
- There must be careful Persuasion: It can't be unexpected.
- Ultimately, a person must be the one to choose. Persuasion is not a question of intimidation, but a suggestion.
- Individuals will tell you through different media styles in all sorts of ways.

1.4 Persuasion Throughout History

We have been persuasive since man first invented a language. Various tribes also persuaded other tribes to join forces or trade-in food. Many wars were caused by persuasion. With that said, persuasion has changed its methods throughout history, while the concept remains the same.

Many persuasive messages we've received have been grown There were not many effective ways to communicate with the public just a hundred years ago. Today, you sign in to social media and see ads on advertisements, or individuals trying to convince you to believe what they believe. Due to the advent of technology, persuasion can fly far quicker. Of course, when people had access to radio, they used it for their benefit. This has helped them transmit like never before a persuasive message Advertising agency in particular. An advertisement's aim is to get you to buy the product or share their ideology, and to do so; an advertiser will use multiple ways to talk to as many people as possible.

Persuasion is more complex in modern times than it used to be. Consumers don't like being overtly marketed, so an organization needs to learn how to get the idea across in a manner that doesn't feel pushy or promoted. If businesses want to persuade somebody, gentle metaphors and recommendations are required.

Persuasion is also harder because everybody is fighting on the Web to get their reputation out. One wants to convince you to buy their product over someone else's product.

1.5 Why persuasion matters

Three reasons why persuasion should be studied by people.   Persuasion: Theory, research, and practice are integrated. First, you will be more successful in persuading others when you study and understand persuasion. You need to have a working understanding of how persuasion works if you want to be a convincing public speaker.

Second, people will be better users of knowledge because they understand persuasion. We live in a society where numerous sources of message are constantly fighting for our attention, as mentioned above. Unfortunately, most people just let them wash messages like a wave over them, making little effort to understand or analyze them. As a result, for half-truths, illogical arguments, and lies, they are more likely to fall. Once you begin to understand persuasion, you will have the ability to pick out the messages sent to you and see why some of them are successful, and others are clearly not.

Eventually, once we understand how persuasion works, we will have a clearer understanding of what is happening in the world around us. We're going to be able to analyze why some speakers are effective persuaders and not others. We will be able to understand why some speakers are able to get an audience eating out of their hands while others are flopping.

In fact, we conclude that being persuasively literate in the twenty-first century is an ethical imperative. We agree that misleading messages aimed at manipulating, pressuring, and intimidating people are immoral, just as messages distorting facts are. It is our duty as moral listeners to examine messages that deceive, coerce, and/or intimidate people or misrepresent data. We are also responsible for battling these messages with the facts, which will ultimately depend on our own skill and experience as successful persuaders.

1.6 Types of Persuasion

Persuasion is a useful tool, whether you are delivering a doctoral thesis or just trying to persuade your spouse to buy a new family room rug. It is important to know the six types of persuasion and how they contribute to presenting your case and winning. They are ethos, pathos, logos, statistics, refutation, and deliberation.

Ethos:

It is related to morality and ethics. Writers or speakers persuade their viewers of their sincerity in this form of persuasion and show themselves as trustworthy. To know whether a writer is credible or not, the audience must understand his intention and a strong understanding of the subject.

Logos:

Logos arises from intuition, and writers utilize science, inference, and insight to persuade readers about their perspective.

Pathos:

The third method is pathos, invoking, and referring to the audience's feelings. This is opposed to logos, as without utilizing logic or reasoning, it makes claims. Many writers perceive love, fear, empathy, and anger as powerful factors that influence their audiences ' emotions.

Statistics:

The fourth form, statistics, is a more advanced process. It is based on the oratories of Greek philosophers and adds to the more advanced scientific knowledge or what we call' hard data.' The key is to differentiate between and how to use statistics and facts. Most views are backed by the phrase "studies show," when the figures collected from a survey often do not actually represent the overall point of the research to support a particular reason or argument.

Deliberation:

Deliberation is one of the two kinds of persuasion proposed by the Greek philosopher Aristotle in his speech. This form of persuasion, also known as legislative speech, is an attempt to answer questions of policy or interest, and to prioritize problems and suggested solutions

Refutation:

The counterpoint to deliberation is refutation. One form of refutation is the speech of rebuttal. To refute is to overcome the statement of the opposition by adding other facts that reduce the appeal of the assertion of the opposition. The other type is the discourse of refutation. This differs from the rebuttal speech because it seeks to prove that the argument of the opposition is either wrong or incorrect, but instead focuses on the opposition speaker's faulty reasoning or lack of support.

1.7 Simple approaches to persuade people

There are three approaches to persuade people to get what you want them to do. These are very different in the process, as well as in their effects.

Control

What it is like having them as a puppet to gain control over a person. It's not that easy, of course, but the principle remains that you try to control their acts without thinking too much about what they think.

How to gain control of another human, and even if they don't want to do it, they do what you want, you need energy. This may be the authority's power, for example, when a manager directs a subordinate. It can also be money power or learning the identity of an individual or other similar leverage mechanisms. There is another way of doing this by using persuasive methods that distract the conscious mind while making suggestions to the unconscious. Conditioning is another approach that relies on the unconscious mind and is capable of working on both humans and animals.

Problems The problem with control is that we are a smart species, and when people try to control us, we don't stop thinking. In fact, as we figure out what is going on and what to do about it, we tend to think harder. We need a sense of control, and when we realize that others are trying to control us, we often get upset and resist their efforts, fight back, or take sly revenge. It makes manipulating persuasion risky and better done only when the other approaches become inefficient.

Convince

What Convincing people are trying to get their consent, get them to care about what's being said, and decide that it's both important and the best choice for them. They will act in aligned ways that seem sensible when people agree. They need less ongoing management and will endeavor to maintain their agreement.

How you need to get their focus and convince them, so they'll listen. Then a convincing argument must be created that presents your case and negates alternative views. You want them to consider and understand, usually in order to act on this respect in the future instead of just taking immediate action (which is where the emphasis of control is). For justifying, you need to prove that your statement is valid, with sufficient reasoning and clarification of cause and effect. Often, a statement becomes more compelling when the person sees how it impacts them individually and influences their desires and goals. Conviction often makes substantial use of language, and word care is needed. The ancient Greeks were practitioners of argument, and in courtrooms and other structured settings, their techniques can still be seen today. Although salespeople are using some risky approaches, they are also trying to persuade, especially when dealing with a company and other repeat customers who may then wonder about how they were convinced.

Problems It is much harder to convince others than simply applying commands. You have to learn about how others thought and be a therapist as well as a linguist and logician to some degree. Although it may work well to convince, it may not be enough. Emotion is the confounding factor that stems the logician. We think less when we are upset, and when we are highly emotional, we lack our reasoning nearly completely.

Convert

What conversion seeks to change the beliefs and values of a person so that they can truly buy into what is suggested so that they can connect emotionally and even change their sense of identity.

How often conversion uses more methods based on emotion than the cooler logic of trying to persuade people. Conversion's emotional aspect suggests it's a more social activity, and it can be very helpful to find opportunities to communicate with the desired individual. Building a relationship is a traditional way to do this. Natural methods like storytelling are aimed at getting people to connect in the tale with idealized characters. These can be turned into a dialogue or used as stories for teaching individually. Many cults use violent methods of conversion to kill and reconstruct the individual, such as isolation and breaking sessions. There are other ways to engage and aspire. Although cult practices sound extreme, in more traditional religions and industries, more humane variations of their tactics can be seen. You may want to discredit the cause rather than the conviction when a person's beliefs come from another individual or origin. Show the source with a shaky foundation as losing legitimacy.

Problems It can be quicker and difficult to persuade than to convince. Individuals also keep their beliefs and values closely and do not easily change. On the other hand, emotional appeals that do not require complex reasoning can convert us. It is especially difficult to change what a person believes when they stick on to that ideology and when it is correlated with other values because targeting a specific conviction is challenging the entire system. This is what occurs when attacking one part of a country. Studies of the cult have shown that although they can trigger very specific values to be accepted by an individual, these results diminish as they escape the world of maintaining cult. What we believe is closely related to the beliefs of the people around us.

Discussion

The most common form of persuasion is control (thinking family, bosses, military), although it is the least effective method of changing minds. This is presumably because it's quickest and simplest if you have the strength you like. It takes more skill to convince and convert, which relatively few people have. These are equivalent to another three-fold: The Three Hs, or Head, Hands, and Heart. Power guides the eyes, letting things happen to people without caring about what they say. Convincing involves the head and asks them to think and agree. Conversion is moving to the core, hoping for an emotional buy-in. When you were to be pessimistic, you could term it' the three drawbacks.' They are a very real choice in practice, and it can be critical to understanding the distinction.

1.8 Function of Persuasion

The most common literary technique is persuasion. We find it not only in literature but also in speeches, conferences, courtrooms, and advertising. Writers convey their own feelings and opinions by persuasive writing personally and rationally speaking to the reader. So, attracting readers or viewers is a very effective technique. It also helps students to uncover those arguments in favor of their points of view and gives them the opportunity to examine evidence similar to their beliefs. By developing an appreciation of how writing can alter their thoughts and actions and affect them, students can understand the nature of persuasive research.

1.9 persuasion skills

One of the most significant skills of persuasion is confidence and commitment. For others to trust you, you have to believe in yourself. There is no magic wand for trust but adequate knowledge of the topic you want to discuss with the other person, smart dressing, and the point-speaking. For example, a marketing executive selling mobile phones to potential customers needs to know comprehensive telecommunications specs, technology, cost, available colors, and so on to persuade them and affect their decision as well. The style in which you market and present your products or services would definitely make the difference in a layman's language. Never force anyone to agree with what you're saying. Leave him / her time to think and return later to you. Surely convincing doesn't mean sitting on someone's chest and pursuing him/her every day.

Make yourself updated with the latest developments in your field so that even the trickiest question can be resolved.

For others, set an example. One must have the "X factor" to affect the decisions, mood, mentality, and so on of others. Let me give you a hypothetical case study: if you are asked to address a crowd of hundreds and persuade them to invest in the products of your organization, what would you do first? Believe me, the first and most important thing to do in such a case is to dress properly. The first experience, so they claim, may not be the last one, but it is the lasting impression. Trust me, if you're dressed up to turn heads, half of your work is done. Avoid being creepy, forgetting to believe, as no one would even bother to look at you.

Believe what you're saying. It's very easy to read others, but the trick is to do the exact stuff you expect from others. Practice what you're teaching. As a boss, if you want to convince someone to get to the workplace on time, you need to make sure that you do the same as well. Unless he uses the same brand at home, a marketing executive would never be able to sell his organization's laptops. There would not be trust. Stay positive because people don't like to communicate and support those who have lost all hope for life themselves. Keep your face with a smile. It is good! Build yourself an aura. Let others be motivated by you.

1.10 persuasion skills that make every person agree with you

It all begins with your planning skills. Your ability to successfully persuade people only when preparation depends on them. Without preparation, nothing can be done. Having adequate information about the people and situations around you is the most important thing. Adequate preparation enables persuasion to be effective.

Instead of rushing right to the end of your point, Jeff Haden suggests, begin with claims or assumptions that your audience can identify with. Develop a framework for further

cooperation. Remember, a body in motion remains to stay in motion, which also applies to a head nodding in agreement.

Storytelling skill

When you try to make a point, telling stories is quite fascinating. Stories have the ability to persuade and influence people. People appear to be paying more interest when reading a story or description rather than showing facts and figures. People will better understand you when demonstrating your concept or approach to them by tales. "Stories are often more persuading than simple statements of fact," says Martin Zwilling. The potential impact is even higher if you can incorporate the recipient explicitly into the story.

Motivating Skill

Persuasion has a strong motivating connection. Without knowing the art of motivation, you can't convince people. It is a difficult task to get people motivated because it depends on personality; the factors that can motivate an individual may differ from those that motivate another. Knowing what allows an individual to become inspired–and stay that way –will help ensure that people are the most effective they can be. Thus, in order to convince people effectively, one should be willing to know what it takes to motivate people.

Problem-solving skill

In our contemporary world, where there are many socio-economic and political problems, individuals with problem-solving skills are highly respected and are able to persuade people to believe in their proposals.

People are constantly searching for problem solvers. Once you have the capacity to dissect problems and find the best alternatives that solved a problem, people will approach you naturally and bow to your persuasive power.

Strategic Thinking Skill

You've often felt that today's world's great inventors and successful businessmen are great thinkers. That's why they were willing to have a big effect on individuals. Warren Buffett is known world's most successful creators by most people; Mark Zuckerberg is

Facebook's chairman, chief executive, and co-founder; while he founded Microsoft, the world's largest software business. These guys, because they are tactical thinkers, are great today. We can easily persuade people to adopt their concepts with this ability.

Confidence

Trust is a requirement for persuasion. If people perceive you lack self-confidence, nobody will ever look at your ideas, views, and opinions. If you really trust in yourself and what you are doing, you will always be able to persuade someone to do what is best to them, while at the same time getting exactly what you want.

Listening Skills

Attentive audiences become influential people. We tend to pay heed to every issue and conversation that naturally makes people love them. Have you ever asked why most people usually say,' thank you for having ears?' We are grateful that someone has been able to listen to their concerns. You will easily influence them by acquiring their trust.

Charisma

Charisma is about what you do and does as opposed to who you really are as a person. The personality, social signals, facial appearance, and how you perceive others all play a role in your charisma growth. Charisma is a powerful influence. You can have a major influence on them when people like you naturally because of how you speak, your composure, calm personality, attitude, etc.

Rapport Skill

Rapport skills are essential to establishing shared trust and friendship with someone or a group of people. Once you have a good interpersonal relationship with someone or a group of people, this gives you the opportunity to relate to them and share some ideas and values. Jason Nazr says,' by mirroring and copying certain typical habits (speech of the body, cadence, rhythms of expression, etc.), you will develop a sense of connection where others feel more comfortable with you and become more responsive to your suggestions.

Loyalty

You will often hear people say,' respect is earned rather than demanded.' This is because people expect those; they admire to behave themselves first and foremost in an orderly manner. You must be trustworthy in order to be able to attract the attention of others that you want to affect.

Research skill

To communicate perfectly and with a command on a subject, a person who wishes to have the power to persuade must be a good researcher. You will be able to explore unlimited knowledge of the points, ideas, and views that you want to convey by having a research skill. The vast knowledge rate offers you an additional advantage in getting others to trust in your concepts.

Human relation skill

The ability of human relationships is critical to persuasion. The traditional theories of leadership struggled partially because they ignored the method of human relations to the supervision of workers. You should be able to understand the pain and problems of a person to be a powerful persuader.

Communication skill

Communication is very necessary if you want to persuade someone or a group of people effectively. It should be a two-way communication that invites reviews. The essence of persuasion rest lies in dialogue and inspiring reactions to discern the state of mind, intentions, and views of the people you want to convince to follow a particular course effectively.

Languages Skills

In the result of globalization, we tend to meet the different languages, value systems, norms, and cultures of people from different nations. Knowing and understanding their languages is one way to establish a social partnership with them. Constant communication with them will encourage you to express your thoughts and impact their opinions.

Mentoring skill

Mentors were generally respected by prodigies in particular. Using mentoring ability is not challenging. Just get people around and express your values, thoughts, and ambitions with them. Certainly, they will be persuaded to join the program so soon as you excel in what you are doing.

Critical Skill

Reasoning is a critical thinking tool. When you don't know anything about them, you don't hope to persuade people. Critical thinking makes you an active learner, not a passive information recipient. Critical thinkers use observation, analysis, interpretation, reflection, evaluation, inference and explanation to make people believe in public speaking skills to be successful in persuading people

Public speaking skill

The art of public speaking must be learned thoroughly. Many people are going to die rather than be on stage and tell the crowd regardless of the size. Public speaking requires trust, scheduling, testing, concentration, narration, audience observation, and much more. These and more make up the ability to speak to the public. Public speaking abilities are, therefore, a requirement to effective convincing.

Public Relations skill

 The art of persuasion requires skill in public relations, especially when one is a public figure. Here versatility, boldness, and adaptability are the attributes that we need to persuade people effectively.

Collaborative skill

Unless there is an ability to cooperate, two or three people cannot function together. Collaborative abilities are habits that enable two or more participants in the group to function together and perform well. By actually knowing them, you can't influence others. Collaborating with them is one way to know and understand people.

Creative skill

You have to be super good at bringing something new into being or setting up a whole new exciting way of doing things to attract the attention of people. It is generally respected by creative thinkers, and people want to associate with them. According to Linda Naiman, founder of Creativity at Work, organizations led by creative leaders have a higher success rate in innovation, employee engagement, change, and renewal.

Decision Making Skills

We daily practice decision making in our lives. Most of these skills depend on the decision-making process. Of starters, selecting the group of people you want to convince, selecting the type of message you want to convey, and selecting the strategies and techniques you want to reassure them are decision-making functions. Without this capacity, while trying to persuade people, one can't achieve anything.

Chapter 2: Difference b/w persuasion and negotiation

2.1 What is Negotiation?

Negotiation is a way of resolving differences. It is a mechanism through which consensus or agreement is achieved while disagreements and conflicts are avoided.

In any conflict, people understandably try to accomplish the best result (or perhaps an entity they represent) for their status. However, the foundations for a successful result are the core values of fairness, mutual benefit, and maintenance of a relationship.

In many situations, specific types of negotiation are being used: in international affairs, law, administration, industrial disputes, or intra-regional relations. But in a variety of activities, overall negotiation skills could be managed to learn and applied. Negotiation experience can help solve the conflicts between you and anyone.

2.2 Negotiation phases

A formal negotiation strategy can be beneficial in securing a favorable outcome. In a job situation, for instance, it may be appropriate to schedule a conference where all the parties concerned will interact.

The negotiation process contains the following phases:

- Preparedness.
- Talk of the matter.
- Objectives clarity.
- Negotiate for the Win-Win results.
- Agreement.
- A course of action to be followed.

1. Preparedness.

A decision must be made before any discussions about when and where to discuss the issue and who will be involved. It is also beneficial to establish a limited time period to avoid more conflicts. This phase involves making sure all the applicable facts are known to explain your position. In the above example, the knowledge of your organization's "rules" for which assistance is given is included when aid is not deemed appropriate and the reasons for such refusals. The rules you can adhere to in preparing talks may be in the organization. While addressing the dispute, planning can help prevent future disagreements and unintentionally waste time during the session.

2. Talk of the matter.

Individuals or representatives of each side put the case as they choose, i.e., their awareness of the situation, forward during this stage. In this step, key skills involve interviewing, listening, and explanation. It is sometimes helpful to note all points raised during the debate stage if further clarification is necessary. Listening is extremely important, as it is simple to make the error that you talk too much and listen too little when there is conflict. Each hand should have the same chance of presenting its case.

3. Objectives clarity.

The aims, interests, and views of the two fronts of the dispute must be clarified from the discussion. Such considerations should be identified as objectives. Through this explanation, certain mutual respect can often be found or created. Clarification is an integral part of the negotiation phase. Unless it is overlooked, difficulties and challenges to obtaining a positive outcome can occur.

4. Discuss the Win-Win results.

In this phase, what is called a win-win in outcome is focused on where the two parties feel their views are considered. This phase concentrates on what is called a win-win output. Generally, the best result is a win-win outcome. It may not always be feasible, but this should be the final goal through mediation. Various strategies and sacrifices suggestions need to be considered here. Commitments are often positive choices, which are often more beneficial than holding the initial positions for all concerned.

5. Agreement.

Accord can be established after attention has been extended to recognizing the opinions and desires of both parties. In order to reach an acceptable outcome, it is necessary that everyone concerned remain open-minded. Any contract must be made absolutely clear so that the decisions have been taken on both sides.

6. A course of action to be followed.

The intervention plan must be followed to carry out the determination under the Agreement.

Non-agreement.

If the negotiation process breaks down, and no agreement is reached, another meeting is expected. It prohibits both sides from engulfing themselves in warm debates or disputes that not only bother wasting time but can also affect future interactions. The negotiation phases should always be repeated at the next meeting. Some new ideas or desires must be addressed, and the condition revisited. It could also be useful at this point to look at alternatives and/or to mediate in another individual.

Informal discussions.

Sometimes, more unofficially, it is necessary to negotiate. In those cases, it might be difficult or necessary to take the above steps officially if there is a disagreement. However, in a variety of casual settings, it can be very helpful to remember the main points in the stage of formal negotiations.

The following three components are important and will likely affect the final outcome of negotiations in any talks:

- Attitudes.

- Awareness.

- Interpersonal competencies.

1. Attitudes

The attitudes to the system itself, for instance, attitudes towards problems and individuals involved with the individual case or attitudes aligned with social acknowledgment requirements, have strongly influenced all discussions. Know always that: mediation is not a place for personal successes to be accomplished. The need to bargain with the government can be resentful. Through bargaining, characteristics may affect the actions of a human, such as that of individuals.

2. Awareness.

The more awareness you have of the issues concerned, the greater your involvement in the negotiation process. Well-preparedness is essential, in other words.

Gain as much knowledge about your assignments as possible about the issues. Therefore, it is essential to understand how things are resolved because mediation in various situations can require different approaches.

3. Interpersonal competencies.

To successful talks, both informal settings and in non-formal or less formal or one-to-one meetings, strong interpersonal skills are important.

Such competencies include:

- Successful verbal contact.

- Hearing.

- Project study.

- Solving question.

- I am deciding.

- Stability.

- Tackling difficult circumstances.

2.3 Are negotiation and persuasion the same?

Negotiation is defined as two, or even more, people interact to reach an agreement on one or more issues and also to talk with another person to arrive at an agreement.

Persuasion can be described as the act or method of manipulating, or of moving to a new opinion, place, or course of action–through argument or intercession. It is key to all discussions to transfer somebody to a new post or action path. Throughout immobilization negotiations, two parties try to find a compromise. This is particularly the case. While anyone may try to negotiate, an efficient and persuasive negotiator typically works more successfully.

Bringing up persuasion as a strategy of negotiation means looking at the various types of conviction values that relate to property transactions. There are six different opportunities for self-interest, individuality, comparison, swap, sameness, and logical sense in property negotiations.

In a perfect world, everybody would agree with you, and you would still be correct. About 99 percent of the time is not like that. What are you doing? Frequently people use manipulation to manipulate their stance on the other side. Persuasion is perfect if it succeeds because it does not cost you much but often does not succeed so that you may have to bargain. So, what the distinction between persuasion and bargaining is.

It is best to switch to a dictionary to describe persuasion, and the meaning' to persuade' of Merriam-Webster is' to compel (somebody) to do something by questioning, debating and/or giving reasons.'

A brilliant short book called "Eristic Dialectic, the Art of Being Wrong" has been published by Arthur Schopenhauer and is still one of the popular rhetoric's of the day. Its 38 stratagems educate you about using logical errors, false proposals, generalization, and other handy instruments. In both processes, there are some important differences: the point of persuasion is to say, and trade is a negotiation. Strategies of persuasion are to explain, to promote, to manipulate, to inspire, to argue, to advise, and to contest.

Negotiation implies, on the other hand, that concerns, desires, shortcomings, motivations, and goals can be discussed, so that a better understanding can be made available from both sides. There is not strictly exclusive convincing and mediation either.

Both could be close to their results or goal. All strategies are very successful, and citizens are often persuaded that they prefer their own reasoning and beliefs above compromise. The other party's reasoning and views tend to us not to be particularly interested. The individual may find it difficult to change his position, but we still choose it as persuading is which we've developed with since childhood and used again. Negotiation is challenging because we really must be attentive to the other party's views, values, and reasoning and therefore consider ways of dealing with them.

If we speak about compromise, there is some uncertainty about whether we say mediation or coercion. Negotiations, in their very essence, warrant a rapprochement between the two sides to reach a compromise. Convincing or manipulating, though, is the process of making the other party do what they want.

The art of convincing is often termed negotiation.

Good negotiation leverage You will learn when and how to use convincing skills to be a good negotiator. This is probably happening at times when you seem unable to agree on negotiations. In these cases, it is also necessary to understand how and when to persuade efficiently.

Use of queries to help persuade others to compromise.

Comments are high as they speak to the other arm. Yet reacting to what is being said is the real art of interrogation. This doesn't mean that you hang on each word. "The detection, selection, and interpretation of keywords that turn information into intelligence," is the definition of Mullender's listening. His conceptual model is' information you use for your benefit.'

In sale's situations, implied and explicit requirements are the keywords that a customer of our SPIN ® Selling Skills model would listen to. An effective sales representative is someone who can turn that information in the form of profit statements into intelligence.

The profit statement requires that sellers dive into issues or perceived concerns, which is precisely the same as that recommended by Mullender to "steer anxiety" in circumstances of recovery. You will define the specific desires (what other side wants to do about this) and render helpful suggestions only by finding the real source of the pain. Unsurprisingly, in these cases, Mullender points to SPIN ® as a "stunningly clever" template.

Ultimately, while talks can be seen as a separate part of a process and a different ability to sell/persuade, a successful leader must still be willing in a negotiating scenario to execute suitable persuasive techniques. They recommend that negotiators develop strong selling strategies and negotiation skills to help them produce win-win outcomes. This is why they support

What should I select?

Seek first to convince and see whether it fits for you. I'm positive, though, we were all on the other hand of someone who told us constantly that we just don't approve. It can be quite annoying. Although persuading and bargaining, know when you hit an impasse.

The Influence of sound is always stronger than the power of language. When you have the point of no-return, substitute the tone to be more convincing or switch your bargaining dialog — you are much more likely to get a response. The Influence of sound is always better than the influence of words.

Chapter 3: Theories and Types of Persuasion

What are we talking about when we are talking about conversions? How can we use ten psychological theories to convince people?

Much of the time, as we speak about converts, we discuss ways we can be much more compelling and successful. We are interested in meeting and doing it in a way that really speaks to customers, fans, and followers. And, how should you persuade, i.e., to convert?

In order to discuss the public, it is very crucial to understand how people are persuaded. Thankfully, a number of scientists have developed theories to explain the factors behind this conviction. Although there are many theories to explain persuasion, we will examine three here only: the theory of social justice, the theory of cognitive dissonance, and the model of probability development.

3.1 Social Judgement Theory

Muzafer Sherif and Carl Hovland (1980) have developed social judgment theory in order to identify the types of communicative messages and the conditions in which conveyed messages will lead to a change in the behavior of somebody, by comparison with the current behavior. Sherif and Hovland essentially discovered that there are people's views of attitudes, values, beliefs, and behaviors on a spectrum such as latitude of rejection, the latitude of non-commitment, and latitude of acceptance.

The persuasive messages found Sherif and Hovland most likely succeeded when they were accepted by the individual. For instance, if you speak about Master in a foreign language, you are more likely to assess your message positively, to assimilate your advice to your own ideas, and to engage in your desired behavior. In addition, it is more likely that people who oppose your message would judge your message negatively and not assimilate your suggestions or participate in the required actions.

We would always be convincing people, in a perfect world, who agree with our views, but this is not a reality. We also find ourselves in positions where we try to convince others to beliefs, principles, opinions, and habits. To help us convince people, the different possible attitudes, values, beliefs, and conducts that exist are what we need to think about. We may, say, see the following potential views from our audience members in a foreign language situation, where students are convinced that they are to be included in this subject:

- **Full agreement.** In foreign languages, let's all be big.

- **Strong consensus.** In a foreign language, I won't be majoring, but in a foreign language, I will double major.

- **Part of the agreement**. I'm not going to make big in a foreign language, but in a foreign language, I'm going to become tiny.

- **Neutral.** While I think it can be helpful to learn a foreign language, I do agree that university education can be achieved without it. But I don't really feel strong in one way or another.

- **Partly discrepancy**. I only take my major foreign language classes.

- **Substantial dispute**. No foreign language courses I do not think I should take.

- **Full dissension**. Maintenance is a complete waste of college education in an alien language.

The seven possible views on the matter do not represent the whole range of choices but concur with the subject in various degrees. So, what does persuasion have to do? Okay, we are glad you asked about this. Sherif and Hovland theoretician the belief that the difference or difference between the speaker and that of the audience is a case of knowing how great it is. If the views of the speaker were like those of the audience, there was more likely to be persuasion. If the difference between the speaker's idea and the listeners is too big, the probability of persuasion is drastically decreasing.

3.2 Cognitive dissonance Theory

In 1957, Leon Festinger suggested another theory to understand the function of persuasion. The cognitive theory of dissonance is an aversive motivating state when an individual simultaneously has two or even more paradoxical attitudes, values, beliefs, or conduct. You might realize, for instance, you ought to focus on your voice, but you really want a buddy to go to a film. In this case, the practice of your speech and the cinema are two different cognitions. The objective of convincing is to induce sufficient dissonance among listeners to alter their attitudes, values, beliefs, or behaviors. Frymier and Nadler (2013) pointed out that three necessary conditions exist for cognitive dissonance to function effectively: affective consequences, freedom of choice, and insufficient outside justification.

Firstly, for cognitive dissonance to work, the consequences or punishment must be strong enough to not change one's own attitudes, values, convictions, or comportment. For example, you might talk about why more apples must be eaten. If your irritating effects are that you won't eat fruit, most viewers won't be convinced of the penalty because your audience won't get enough food. Instead, the penalty correlated with not eating apples must be sufficiently important to change behavior for cognitive dissonance to work. If you persuade your audience that they are at a higher risk of heart disease or colon cancer with too little fiber in their nutrition, you may be sufficiently afraid to change behavior.

The second criterion that people have freedom of choice for cognitive dissonance in their jobs. If listeners feel compelled to do something, dissonance will not arise. We can change their behavior quickly, but the original behavior may reappear as soon as the manipulation is finished. This is like driving slower when a policeman is in the vicinity but ignores speed limits as soon as the personnel is no longer present. You, as a presenter, have to guarantee that your viewer doesn't feel obligated nor coerced if you want to raise cognitive dissonance, but that they can easily see that they have the option to be convinced.

The ultimate condition for cognitive dissonance is internal and external justifications. The external reasoning refers to the process of determining why one's behavior, beliefs, and attitudes are outside one's control. Internal justification comes with a person willingly modifying a cognitive dissonance behavior, belief, or attitude. External justifications are far less likely to cause changes through persuasion than internal justifications.

Maybe not unexpectedly, the psychology starts with hacking for transformation and convincing. To understand why anyone interacts or why they respond, you need to look at the wired nature of the user and how we all are wired. It helps to understand how people think and feel in order to understand persuasion and the social media influence, to focus and to love conversion. This is the first.

3.3 The Use Psychological Theories of Persuasion

Here's a concise rundown of all ten theories that could seem really similar to you—either because you used them in the past, or because you had someone using them on you. Here's a brief overview of each hypothesis.

1. Hypothesis of improvement.

When you convey a particular attitude with confidence, that attitude will become more complicated. The contrary is true: the mindset is silenced when voicing confusion.

2. Theory of conversion

The minority in a team will affect the majority overwhelmingly. Usually, the most vulnerable in the majority are those who can enter because it was simple or because there were no substitutes. The most powerful are strong, trustworthy minority voices.

3. Theory of information manipulation.

The theory requires a persuasive person who intentionally violates one of the four maxims of speech.

The four are:

- Quantity: full and complete information.

- Quality: truthful and accurate data.

- Relationship: The data is of conversation relevance.

- Manner: the data is conveyed quickly, and the voice of claim four is accompanied by non-verbal actions.

4. Priming

Stimuli that impact how you view short-term actions and thoughts will control you. Here is a really insightful example from Changing Minds. A stage magician suggests, in separate sentences, "tried" and "cycled" as he starts an individual to then think about "trickle."

5. The practice of reciprocity.

Reciprocity, a shared social norm, requires the responsibility to share the gains of other citizens.

6. Principle of Scarcity.

What is missing is what you want. The drive grows when you expect your disappointment should you struggle to do so rapidly.

7. Effect of sleeper.

Convincing advertisements tend to reduce conviction over time, except for outlets with low credence. Messages starting with low-conveniently gain insight as to our brains slowly separate the origin of the content (i.e., a seemingly sleazy vehicle dealer and his suggestions on what car is best).

8. Social impact.

Based on the way we view the interaction with the influencer, certain individuals affect us strongly. For example, social data on-site copy is compelling if the information and advice are from reputable sources, big retailers, or other individuals.

9. Approach: Yale Attitude Change.

On the basis of several years of Yale University research, this approach has identified a number of considerations in persuasive speech, including the fact that it has become a credible and attractive speaker, whether first or last; and the ideal population to focus.

10. Ultimate Conditions.

Many terms have more influence than others. The principle splits into three groups convincing terms: God's words: certain phrases that bring blessings or warrant obedience. E.g., improvement, quality Devil words: certain phrases which are disdainful and deter. For example, authoritarian, pedophile language: certain terms that are abstract, less known than either the words' god' or' devil.' For example, equality, commitment These ten principles could be viewed as the foundations of the convincing tactics listed below.

3.4 Here's for the thing we all crave

We all understand how important food, water, refuge, and warmth are for our survival. Any thoughts, what's the most important next? The hierarchy of the psychiatrist Abraham Maslow's 1940s hierarchy of needs reveals the advanced level of how we have desires on the road to success. The version of the pyramid below shows five different levels of needs (shared by the Doorway project). The most important approach is advertising in three stages between physical conditions and fulfillment requires.

In the hierarchy of Maslow, definitions of these criteria don't have an exact advertising viewpoint, so it takes a bit of imagination and see how you can respond to these needs. The author and expert in the field of persuasion, Jristine Comaford, has found security, belonging, and appreciation to a tremendous value for our daily work and our innovative lives: Without such three important keys a person can't perform, innovate, engage emotionally, agree on or move on...

Her experience helped her to formulate three sentences which are key to influence and conviction and to build this sense of security, belonging, and importance that we all need. That statement excludes arrogance from the discussion, creating an environment that is healthy for imagination and brainstorming. This expression is "what if." "I want your help." This reverses the dominant, subordinate roles, involves, and transfers power to another person. That statement shifts the emphasis from the question to the answer. "Will it be beneficial if."

Here is an illustration from the SEO Nick, who uses explicitly in an email the expression "I need your support." HOW TO WIN WIN Colleagues AND INFLUENCE YOUR AUDIENCE. We hear you talk to influencing people; we listen to Buffer. (I think each one of these three would be fun to try out email lines.) Dale Carnegie's book How to Keep Friends and People with Power is the foundation for our business values and culture. The famous circle of Carnegie has the guidance from Christine Comaford above. Disable your ego. Bliss and positiveness standard.

In many respects, Carnegie's Book could begin and finish a debate regarding persuasion and power. Here's just a page of the contents of the novel, full of fun, helpful, partnering concepts. (Carnegie would certainly not like to see you just read the contents table—he urged the reader to read every paragraph in his book several times.) It is only possible to avoid the best argument.

Express conformity with the views of the other party. Don't say, "You're wrong." Recognize it rapidly and strongly if you are wrong.

- Enter in a polite manner.

- Immediately have the other person to say, "yes, yes."

- Just let the other individual talk a lot.

- Just let the person feel his or her idea.

- Look at things frankly from the viewpoint of the other guy.

- Convince yourself of the thoughts and expectations of another human.

- The nobler intentions were challenged.

- Screen your thoughts.

- Put a question away.

3.5 The Persuasion Drop

How to react at persuasion: as a sandbox drop. Here's a nice way to look at it.

The idea is based on Roger Dooley of the Neuromarketing blog that uses a person's variables on a slide to show how important influences influence the results. Here's the diagram he generated to illustrate the idea: basically, it functions like this: you're offering a customer a lift (a message, a blog article, a phone call, an advertisement).

The magnitude, the inner motives of the client, allow the consumer to push the slip back.

Extra motivation (slide angle) that you provide can improve gravity. If a person has a low internal drive, he or she will choose a steeper path.

Friction here seen as the (real and perceived) difficulties in transforming allows the diaphragm to lag in different degrees. The blow can be most convincing, for instance, a few of our above-mentioned psychological theories. An extension can further strengthen the customer's values and attitudes when he falls down the slide. Social evidence could push the slide further down, resulting in a quicker conversion.

3.6 Persuasion Opportunities

You already realize how much intuition is important with persuasive performance. In addition, psychology can be seen in social networking messages and marketing techniques of certain influential brands. When it comes to the application of the concepts of persuasive psychology, you can start here in a few places.

- The names.
- The news and messages.
- Your contacts.
- Descriptions of your items.

You can become an incentive to justify almost everywhere you have words or visuals–everywhere you produce or handle information.

3.7 Types of Persuasion

There are growing Persuasion values or kinds. Different kinds of persuasion can persuade persons in various ways. When you have someone, who is truly grounded and can only understand and see, you must use the appeal-to-reason approach while someone who has some more confidence in addressing the appeal-to-emotion form.

1. Appeal to reason is the first kind of persuasion. The form of appeal to justification incorporates a logical argument with a logical and scientific perspective on reasoning. This method works better for those who need evidence which supports claims based on faith rather than truth. This method works well. If you want to influence a group of scientists to believe that the earth revolves around the moon, you need a great deal of evidence to prove it. Otherwise, you will not persuade them to argue. Simply saying that it seems to revolve around the moon is a statement so faith-focused and won't work for both the appeal-to-reason process.

2. An appeal for emotion is the second category of persuasion. The appeal to emotion may not be based on evidence but on feelings. It can often be a more effective method for the entire population, as individuals can often be controlled by their impulses rather than by their brains. Throughout the past, this has been illustrated in several cases. You use the technique of calling to emotion to refer to and pass your confidence and creativity to your own statement. Seduction, rituals, or even empathy may also be used to get them to consent. This method is quite well used by salespeople. By showing you a test drive of a vehicle so you can see yourself in a vehicle, you appeal to your imagination. Occasionally, though, you'll feel sorrowful about how you might need this deal, as it was a slow month. Many people also turn to you with seduction. Propaganda and advertisement are two different examples of using that type of belief. Appealing to feelings is also a way to get someone close to you. "We've already done so in that manner, so we should continue to do so," it often operates very well, even though there are many certain methods available which are more successful than what you seek to get people to agree with.

There are several aids of confidence that can help persuade someone to believe or dream. Not these can be employed in written persuasion, however the more you grasp persuasion, both orally and in prose. These are:

The Body Language. Around two-thirds of our interaction is focused on the language of our bodies. For example, you must stand with your hands, hands out as a symbolic gesture of peace, if you want someone open to your ideas. If you stand with crossed arms, you block the recipient, and you won't want to deal with or listen to you unconsciously.

Ability to communicate. The more you talk and write what you want to know, the more open people you want to say. When you claim, "I'd like to give you the chance to buy my brand," you may not be prepared to purchase due to the extremely poor language and orthography. But if you claim, "I want to give you a chance once in a lifetime to live what it really means always to have spare time with this amazing product!"— Here in most ways, you speak to the guy. Look at different advertisements on the Web to see how it actually functions.

Professional Sales. This method uses simple sales techniques that can be learned over time. Learn how to illustrate only good points, react to the needs of an individual, and more.

Tests of personality. You may develop a strategy based on the type of communication of an entity with personality tests. Most people want to talk to each other via telephone or email. Some tend to buy items on Television, whilst others only buy products if they are required. The personality of that person is responsible for knowing how to sell products or ideas to someone.

Sometimes, but not always as many, or ethically, there are four other strategies used:

Frustration. You could get them to do it if you fool anyone in thinking that your plan is the best choice. This has been achieved by many finance gurus to get investment money through the false profit of the company or its assets.

Hypnotization. In hypnosis, a wide array of things can be persuaded. Nevertheless, published justification does not improve.

Advertisement Subliminal. Films successfully use this by inserting items in the context to make viewers watch the film. Cast Away was described as a long commercial by FedEx because of its background use of FedEx products.

Strength. Those who think they are in charge respond positively. It's much simpler to get somebody to follow your desire by faking power or giving an image of power. A courier will send a note to the building that requires people to stop coffee without having to pay for it. The CEO will do so without hesitation, though.

Cause and feeling awareness

They need to fully understand the concepts of rationality and feeling and learn how to write good convictions. At the outset of this cycle, we will also glance quickly at the third call to justification, which is a compelling confirmation of one's existence.

Throughout philosophy, the ideas of fact, reasoning, justification, and argument are explored by great philosophers. Aristoteles believed that the appeals to logic, the calls to sentiment, and the appeal to character reside in three types of persuasion. These are the symbols, pathos, and philosophy defined by him.

Logos is a word of the Greek language, which means a lot, including reason, which is the justification for the appeal. Aristotle claimed that this appeal was necessary to carry out every conversation since this was the rational source of conviction. There are no contradictions and no disappointments with such convincing. Everything emerges from proof, science, and logic. The whole is the truth. Descartes, who has said "I think I am," is one of the most well-known arguments for the plea to justify our existence. We know we are alive, we know we dream, and so we realize we remain. There is evidence and no manner to lie. It doesn't matter by claiming, "I guess, that is why I travel." Thinking leads to research, which leads to flight, but this is more in the inspiration of feeling because there are unclear associations between them.

The appeal to reason applies to an individual's internal purpose. Any dispute or conflict on this is abusive. All the appeals for reason are measured and logically presented.

There are two steps in the system of reasoning:

Inference and Induction.

Here is a case in point for an appeal to reason: the question is whether nuclear weapons are or should not be dangerous and prohibited. They should then be excluded, yeah, your position. Therefore, to decide if you can make a good reason and present a persuasive essay concerning this concept, you must ask yourself four questions:

- Do you still have the evidence for your claim?

- Does the evidence you present to your audience trust?

- What are your conclusions, they are logical and fair? What are they?

- Will you say that you comply with your claims?

It takes us to your inference, the premise from which you derive the assumption. Your allowance would be divided into two premises and a conclusion.

The central basis of your argument is that the risk of mutually assured destruction implies that nuclear weapons are negative. The small concept is the acquisition of nuclear weapons by unstable nations. Thus, the world will be devastated by nuclear weapons. That's what you have to do.

Now you must question yourself whether this is a sufficiently strong statement.

- Do your statements support it?
- Does a connection between dangerous nuclear bombs and the destruction of the planet have a cause and effect?

This now leads us to the conclusion that it is based on facts and cases in general. The details are as follows:

- Hiroshima and Nagasaki have been destroyed by nuclear weapons by decades of thousands owing to atomic consequences.
- Today's nuclear weapons are a lot stronger.
- Nuclear weapons are available for nations such as North Korea, Iran, Pakistan, Israel, and India and are found in unstable areas.
- A nuclear war among Pakistan and India could contribute to a worldwide nuclear winter.

You have created an effective argument with these details, the inference and other arguments that nuclear weapons are, therefore, harmful and should be forbidden. You haven't cheated and asked for the excuses of those who listen to you.

Emotional Appeal

The emotional appeal works differently. The Cicero thinker, regarded as pathos, is renowned for his motivation to finish claim or statement with an emotional appeal to get those who listen to agree with your opinions. While it is fantastic if all listened only to rational arguments, the fact is that emotional appeal is extremely effective since people are heavily influenced by their emotions.

Another form that the appeal of feelings is widely used is images. Drivers Education is a good illustration of this. It is not as successful in justifying the risk of drinking and driving in an emotional appeal as a request for empathy that demonstrates the victims of car crashes in drunk driving accidents.

With respect to our explanation of how nuclear weapons are harmful, we could use the following statements.

- Images from Hiroshima and Nagasaki could be shown with survivors of nuclear poisoning.
- The development of small nuclear arms in these areas could be illustrated.
- They will show clips of nuclear weapons and the damage they cause, which blast around the planet.

- The footage of the nuclear bomb-maker Robert Oppenheimer could be shown. Through his grief, he states that he is now the lord, Shiva, the Destroyer of the Worlds.

One might also refer to viewers' feelings through the fear of cancer, and by the intense irradiation that they experienced during the atomic explosion, that people literally made their skin drop.

Protagonist Appeal

Thirdly, the appeal to the protagonist, also recognized as philosophy, is persuading. This persuasion method is established by speech and speech. Aristotle suggests that the persuader wants the person he is trying to persuade to be intelligent and kind to him in order for the quality of his work to appeal. Cicero felt that the first part of a speech had to be the character establishment for the audience.

One of the following must be achieved in a particular argument by appealing to an individual's ethics:

1. Are you a good person?

2. Are you a figure of authority?

3. Are you ethical?

4. Should you care about the audience's well-being?

The viewer will trust the person who talks to them in the appeal of a person's character, or that will not succeed.

Chapter 4: Techniques of Persuasion

4.1 Psychological Persuasion

In a wide range of ways, we face persuasion every day. An average person is subjected to around 600 to 625 advertisements each day, as per Media Matters. Meat producers would like us to purchase their latest products, and film studios would like us to see the newest blockbusters. Because convincing is such an all-round part of our lives, ignoring how we are affected by influences external to us is often far too simple.

However, persuasion is not only helpful to advertisers and salesmen. Learning how to use these techniques in everyday life can help you be a better dealer and increase the likelihood of getting what you want, whether you want to persuade your child to eat her or to convince your boss to raise her.

Because power is so valuable in many areas of everyday life, methods of persuasion have been practiced and experienced because of olden times. Yet social psychologists started to systematically research such robust methods only at the beginning of the 20th century.

4.2 Key Techniques

The ultimate objective of reasoning is to satisfy the intention of internalizing the convincing argument and to accept this new attitude as a central faith system.

These are all just a few of the most effective techniques for convincing. The use of incentives, fines, correct or incorrect knowledge, and many others are many approaches.

Develop a need

Another form of reasoning is to build a need or to cater to an established need. Such kinds of convictions refer to the fundamental needs of an individual for security, affection, self-esteem, and self-recovery. Marketers also sell their goods with this technique. Take, for instance, the number of advertisements that people have to buy a special product to be happy, secure, loved, or admired.

Social Needs Appeal

A need to be famous, influential, or equivalent to others is another very powerful persuasion tool. Television advertisements provide several examples of this kind of persuasion where viewers are invited to buy products so that they can be like anyone else or be like a renowned or respected individual.

TV ads are a major source of convincing because some estimates suggest that American watches range between 1,500 and 2 000 hours per annum for programming.

Use Words & Images Designed

Persuasion utilizes packed words and pictures also often. The publisher is fully aware of the strength of positive words, so many ads use expressions such as "Fresh and Enhanced or "All Normal."

Get "Foot-in-the-Door"

The "foot-in-the-door or" system is another technique, sometimes successful in making people follow an application. This convincing strategy involves putting someone to accept a small request, such as asking them to buy a small product and then to request it much larger. When the requester recognizes the low initial gain, he has his "foot in the door" and is more willing to fulfill the greater query.

For example, a friend asks you to sit down for an hour or two with her two kids. After you approve the smaller demand, she wonders if you can just hold the kids for the remainder of the day. You may feel obliged to accept the great demand as you have already decided to agree with the smaller application. This is an outstanding example of what psychologists call the law of interaction, and advertisers often use its technique to support customers in the purchase of products and services.

Go big and then small

This is the opposite view of the doorway. A salesman starts with a great, often unrealistic demand. The person responds by denying, shutting the door on the selling figuratively. The seller responds by demanding a ton more, which is often conciliatory. People are often compelled to answer these offers. Since they declined this initial application, citizens are often obliged to help the vendor, fulfilling the smaller order.

Use the reciprocal power

Perhaps if people give you a favor, you will be forced to repay the favor. This is recognized as the mutual principle, a moral duty for others to do something since they have done anything for you first. Marketing professionals can use this phenomenon by making it appear that they are kind to you, such as "extras" or bonuses, which then encourages people to accept the product and make a purchase.

Create your negotiations with an anchor point

The anchoring prejudicial is a subtle cognitive prejudicial to negotiation and decisions. The first offer tends to be an anchor across all future negotiations when trying to reach a decision. So, you can help shape the future negotiations on your behalf if you try to negotiate a salary increase and are the first one to suggest a number, especially when the figure is a little high. This first number becomes the point of departure. While this number could not be met, beginning high could result in your boss having a higher offer.

Limited accessibility

Robert Cialdini is known for the six theories of control, which he first identified in his novel, control: the mental influence of persuasion, best-selling in 1984. One of the fundamental principles he defined was called lack or limitation of usability. Cialdini suggests that if they are scarce or limited, things become more attractive.

It is more likely that people will buy something if it is the last or if selling comes to an end soon. Of illustration, an artist could only do a limited print run. Since only a few prints are available for sale, people could buy before they are gone.

Please notice compelling reminders for spending time

The above examples are just some of the many convincing techniques that social psychologists have described. Seek descriptions of persuasion in your everyday experience. A half an hour random TV program is an interesting experiment that requires any single instance of convincing advertising. You could be surprised at the sheer volume of persuasive strategies that have been used in such a short time.

4.3 Persuasion Techniques that change the mind

The most successful people and renowned businesses use these eight persuasion tactics. Such persuasive techniques work on the unconscious and, if grasped and used correctly, will produce top-notch performance. We also analyzed and outlined the best tactics there for pleasure in learning.

Door footstep:

The door footstep indicates that you should negotiate for a tiny one before applying for a huge one. When you first ask for something small, you are committed to helping the individual, and the greater proposal acts as a reversal of something already agreed on technically.

Real-life Implementation: Tourist requests guidance. We suggest that they may get lost and need you to walk there. You agree with that more than if you ask the other question straight away. You lost a class and requested notes from your classmate. You then admit that this semester was very irresponsible and request notes for the whole semester. When you first apply for the tiny favor, the chance of getting the big one improves, a free ride on the notes of your classmate. The professor has not offered a refreshment, and you decide to ask for your feedback and why you have not accompanied by request for a redo. You have only failed. In such a scenario, rather than requesting a recovery, you're more likely to be successful.

Case study: In 1966, Jonathan Freedman and Scott Fraser, two researchers at Stánford, decided on a persuasion test to test FITD's effectiveness. One hundred fifty-six women in four groups were divided. The first three groups were called and asked a few basic questions regarding their household kitchen products. We called for their own kitchen cabinet to go and list their items three days later. Only with the second offer was the other group approached. There was an approval rate of 52.8% for the first three teams, while the last class had only 22.2%.

Door in the face:

 Hey, you'd like to race the roads naked and scream how amazing this chapter is? No? Okay, at least do you post it on Facebook with your buddies? The door to face is the reverse of the above-mentioned method of convincing. First, you ask for anything huge, with which you will not agree, and then ask for something that is, in contrast, easier.

Real-life implementation: You are asking a teacher in Advanced Statistics for your next mid-term. Oh, and until now at all, you haven't studied. The student apologizes and says they just have no time. Moreover, never before have they ever seen you. However, your follow-up application for your notes is allowed. You're telling your mate to lend $100 to you. You ask after the No, "can I have a minimum of $20?" A supermarket has a strategy of requiring a charity donation, before requesting the payment from the customer. Although most of our customers would not give money, the number of donations increases exponentially if the Store manager asks them to donate 100 dollars and ask, "How only about 5 dollars."

Case study: A study of the DITF technique to support retail sales. Case study: In the Austrian Alps, a saleswoman sold cheese to people passing by a hut. The walkers were decided to offer a pound of cheese for 4 euros in the first scenario.

The saleswomen first provided 2 pounds of cheese for 8 Euros in the second scenario, but after rejection, requested a pound for 4. Compliance rates vary dramatically: 9% for the first application, 24% for the second.

Anchoring

In most decision-making processes, anchoring is cognitive bias. For instance, how do you understand what "good" product is? You equate it with a similar item, and from there you determine. This technology has many various uses, among which pricing is most commonly used. If properly used, anchoring may be a strong technique of persuasion.

Real-Life Implementation: You want to buy a new car and consider an okay price for $10,000. You negotiate with the seller, and you can reduce the cost to $7,000. You go home with satisfaction and disdain, thinking about how much a deal it was. However, the actual value was less than $7,000 for the car. You will receive nothing lower than the initial $10,000 deal as an anchor, so you've only got a new job offer and an initial $2,000 monthly offer. It's about $2,200, which you settle. Once, you could become low-balled, as with the earlier example. Although an increase of 10% over the previous offer might seem attractive, it may still be less than your actual value.

Case study: Three separate payment plans were used by the Economist. A) 59 $online printing B) 125 $printing and 125 $printing and web printing. In a 100 MIT study, sixteen chose option A, and 84 chose option C. The experimenter then eliminated Option B and offered the same exam to 100 other participants. Enhance 8 Persuasion tactics to alter everyone's mind 68 selected option A and 32 selected option C in this case.

The takeoff is that people use option B as their anchor. Nobody really would choose it; it was only used to add option C value.

Commitment & Coherence

Principle: People are more prone to behave and believe regularly. You can use the initial promise to persuade an individual to do more for you if you contribute something little.

Real-life implementation: You purchase the same products time and again most of the time. How did you last try a new beverage or snack? "Will you answer me?" You remember." "Can you get me a drink out of the shop? You probably have heard that goal establishing will improve performance. "In comparison," Yeah, you could do, etc. The concept is seldom left out of a book of self-help. It is because of continuity that this is effective: you know more than once you write down this, it's what you want and therefore should strive for. Let's presume you're operating with an NGO, and for some reason, you collect money. You should ask the person to support the cause before asking for money. They would certainly respond favorably if the explanation is right. You are much more likely to receive contributions when posing such a request first.

Case study: A lot of websites now use the principle of consistency to make you register for their email lists. They usually read anything in their pop-ups: "Yes, subscribe to me. Free money, I love it!" And" No, I would like not to win. While it might look a little common, it helps to boost conversion rates.

Social evidence

Principle: This must be real; everybody knows.' Public confirmation is the most compelling tool for argument. It needs little to remember that there is a high degree of group thinking in most social groups. Somebody suggests a concept, and everybody goes with it–even if everyone opposes it. People just look at what their colleagues do and act in the same way before deciding.

Real-life implementation: You can consider filling the pot before beginning the change if you have a bare tip jar at work. Customers are much more likely to give feedback if they see an empty tip jar than a full tip jar, so I should actually be doing the same thing. There is a major chance that you could want a Facebook message if it has lots of likes, rather than a post that has none. Social data is the reason why most people consume cigarettes. Everybody cigarettes, and you ought to drink, even though it's safe and with an awful taste.

Case study: Many participants were put in a dark room 15 inches from a spot of light in 1935 in an observation made by Muzafer Sherif. The issues were then required to determine how much the object was going. There were different numbers both participants sent. On the next day, the same question was asked and put together. This time, the negotiations began, far from the previous estimates, on a completely different level.

Authority

Principle: People look to authority in any area or subject, so it can take you a long way to make yourself a link of authority.

Real-Life application: If they have been mentioned on major media blogs, many businesses or smaller companies place their "as seen on" icon on their landing pages. When, for instance, one business was on TechCrunch, that implies it's a big deal, since TechCrunch doesn't protect just anybody. 9/10 dentists believe the best one is a certain toothpaste product. It also supplies third world countries with clean drinking water. And heal cancer. In their landing page, organizations tend to discuss their predecessors. It refers in addition to large corporations.

Case Study: Where Stanley Milgram, a psychiatrist at Yale University, carried out several psychological studies that were later called Milgram Experiments. The research was conducted in three roles: experimenter, instructor, and subject. The instructor will ask the pupil, the hiring person, questions, who will be the volunteer.

The instructor would deliver an electric shock if the student reacted correctly. Even after the learner "screamed pain," the experimenter continued pushing the teacher to use the electrical shock. In most cases, the teacher only followed the instructions of the experiment, despite being aware that he had caused extreme pain to another man. Even after their students stopped hearing any reaction and assumed that it was over, 8 out of 10 educators proceeded to deliver the shocks. The theft is that most people want to take control over someone, even to do something obviously wrong.

Scarcity

Principle: Scarcity is among the most widely employed salesmen and advertisers' persuasive tactics. People are more likely to want more of the low supply stuff. When you tell others that something is free only for a limited period or that something is in a limited amount, you would rather.

Real-life implementation: Booking.com rarely fails to show how only 2-3 spaces were left in the hotel or how 20 people look at the same hotel. Digital marketing companies use scarcity by providing their goods once a year for a certain period while emphasizing the limited time that the product offers. Similarly, offer a discount, but connect a timer or date of validity. The greater the conversion rate, the more you emphasize how restricted the product is. Let's say that you are the salesman at the door. With this tactic of convincing, you can go pretty wild. You might claim, for instance, that you're just in the region that day or that you do a special promotion that is never to be seen. In other terms, at no other point will the consumer be allowed to purchase the item.

Case study: 180 participants were split into two classes in an experiment carried out by Luigi Mitton and Lucia Savadori. Next, an item was described that was meant to be rare, and the other was an ample commodity. The experiment reached the conclusion that it was less likely for students to select the good that they were told.

Reciprocity

Principle: People are often compelled to give back favors. No matter if the person loves the gift, they are inclined to give something back. It is always helpful to feel indebted to you, raising your chances of getting something you really want exponentially.

Real-Life implementation: suggest you collect money to help kids find a new home. You might plan a small event until you look for potential sponsors, where children make bracelets from different materials (funny, not the kind of child labor). You can give away the bracelet before requesting a donation so that the possible future donor feels obliged. You probably wouldn't do it if I had questioned you to share this information in the introduction. You are more likely to do so now that you have learned all kinds of useful methods of persuasion, as well as various case studies. Okay?

Case study: The more accommodating the waiter appeared, the more the client will pay the experiment carried out in a splendid New York restaurant. The waiter would provide each client with a piece of chocolate in the first case, resulted in an 18% higher tip. In the second, the water will start to walk, turn round, and give the consumer an alternate piece of candy after offering a piece of candy. The result was an increase in the tip to 21%.

Chapter 5: Improving Persuasion Skills

How often did you have to persuade other people to do anything? It is almost regular, whether it's your teenager who is cleaning his house, or your preschooler who is getting dressed or a colleague who is taking part in a meeting. Many people have been able to do this easily and almost without recognizing anyone, while others are unwilling to impose their position. The skills of persuasion can be mastered just like anybody else and are a key component in being able to manipulate others to achieve the objectives.

5.1 Influence & persuasion approaches

Nagging.

We also know people who are always attempting to persuade by chatting. We appear to believe that they can submit to others, simply by constantly repeating their views. That's nagging, practically. And it works, of course, sometimes because your friends or your family just want some quiet. But as a rule, most typically didn't purchase and don't dedicate themselves to the idea in this way. That means that the concept could easily wither and die when it becomes hard.

Coercion.

Others are falling back on their influence and forcing others to make their wishes. This is bullying, in its most disgusting sense. Also, what they do won't necessarily suit their families or colleagues. They could well surrender if it is complicated. Further directives to save the concept will be given. But again, they may not succeed, because those involved have to do it, not just because they have to.

Better method.

The "Holy Grail" of persuasion, therefore, is to make someone adopt the idea and to do it that way. As well as the best way to do this is not to be noticed by others. But how does that happen? A good example of this is the tale of the sun and the moon: the wind and the sun agreed to fight for once to determine who was stronger. The champion will be the one who would persuade a person to remove his coat. The wind blew and blew; however, the guy still held his coat tighter. Then the sun was shining softly, and the guy took off his coat within minutes.

It's true that you can't force people to do what they don't want; instead, persuasion has the ability to make them want what they want.

Take this example of a student group selecting a group leader. There had been two likely candidates in the party, Sue and Steven, decided on an ideal type of person. Sue recommended that Steven take on this role and happily accepted it. Choice made. With the exception of one group member, John, everybody smiled. John said: "Steven do not hesitate to let us know that you want us to be doing to help. John, who had been quiet until that moment. You'll have a lot to do about your new job, and you have to make sure that you plan us, or we don't do it all. "Steven looked serious, then said," You know, I don't know when I think I have time to do that and start my new job, I'm not sure. As you said, I've got a lot going. Everybody looked at Sue, who said she would consider it if the group wanted to. It would perhaps be easier for Sue to do this. Everybody decided that the best thing would be. Sue later privately asked John why he had gotten involved when all the group had determined on a leader beforehand. He said he thought she was going to do it better than Steven and get the team a better score. In this case, John rather strategically used his negotiating skills to get what he wanted and produced a win-win outcome from a potentially disagreeable discussion. Steven was pleased the team remembered his credentials and was equally grateful that he was not leading the mission. He needed Sue to lead it, in fact, in the end, so he didn't have to threaten troubled John by asking Sue to be better.

5.2 Obstacles to effective persuasion

Another way of thinking as to what works to persuade others is to talk about what does not work. Kurt Mortensen mentions ten challenges to positive persuasion in his book Persuasion IQ: Believe that you are much better than you do and, therefore, cannot improve your skills. Take a long and careful look instead and see where you have to improve your skills.

- Too difficult to persuade. Likewise, people are often more quickly put off than anything else.

- Don't try to do what you want. In this universe, something, or at least nothing, is free

- Too much talk. Stop and listen only to the persons you have to convince.

- To provide too much data to confuse people and make them think you want to blind them to science. You're not asking them, they ask? What?

- Be Desperate. Unlike dishonesty, people can and don't like fear at a distance.

- Be scared of rejection. In extreme cases, this can even prevent people from persuading.

- I'm not prepared. Each time you can't wing it. Your audience will see you and believe you appreciate your time more than yours.

- Assume the audience and then not able to reassess if overwhelming evidence emerges.

- Forget about the importance of the whole conversation. You must work to persuade, right from the outset.

5.3 Successful Persuasion

Study shows that people like certain things about good persuaders. Research by Kurt Mortensen shows this as a major emotional element. These include commitments to be trustworthy and accountable, to be sincere, truthful, and honest, to know and believe in their subject, to build up relationships, and be entertaining and to not argue and provide workable solutions. Therefore, the key ability to succeed is quite broad. First, positive persuaders appear to have greater self-esteem and, more usually, good emotional intelligence. You truly think you are going to succeed.

Empathy and good hearing skills, like mindfulness, are main competences here. Normally, once you hear, the audience asks you how and what they think. It helps to build friendships, including people taking time to be a friend and an influencer. That really follows: if we're honest, we will do much better than someone we don't like, although the idea is sensitive. Building relationships can help build trust, so look at our personal motivation page for more on building confidence.

Good people or influencers also have a very great ability to communicate. You must be able to make your point quickly and effectively. Otherwise, you will never persuade anyone about the merits of your work. There is an inherent talent for successful persuaders. You do your homework, you know your audience, and you know your subject. It took you time to plan and reflect on what you want to do.

5.4 Improvement of Persuasion Skills with Following Tips

You may become an outstanding businessman–zeal, determination, work ethics, etc. by these several skills. Yet how well you can convince other people is among the most important elements in your financial success. Sales, strategic partnerships, and even bosses are about persuading others that the company is worth your commitment, be it energy, cash, or both. Do not be panic full: as with any other talent, you will learn and develop your way of persuading, if you are not a normal, charismatic person. Underneath, eight businessmen offer their best tips to be more compelling.

Recognize what the audience is driven.

No matter how large or tiny the market is, the desire to behave is important to successful convincing, says Conscious Lifestyle magazine co-founder and publisher. He advises, "Put yourself in their shoes." "What are your dreams, your desires, your battles, and your frustrations? If you understand these, you could get someone to do anything." Throughout general consumers are pleased by most of their desires, as per Rachel Beider, CEO of PRESS Modern Massage. If you can think of concerns a person did not even know they had, you get more convincing. There are many choices that people make because of fear and uncertainty, and you could win over someone if you add the notion there are unthought needs."

Share a story.

Throughout marketing and sales, storytelling is important. This is why the LFNT Distribution co-founder, Colbey Pfund, believes that telling a story can make yourself more convincing. He said, "It is important to know from where we come and how we do what we are doing. "It reflects the enthusiasm, and it offers people a way to connect. I confronted everybody with what I actually accomplished, how I began, and why I felt it was so important."

Most people believe in a conversation or a sales pitch face to face. Once you send a substantive response to your situation, Codie Sanchez, Cresco Capital Partners president, advises that you write down your thoughts and evaluate them objectively to strengthen your point. "You can't help but master it if you scatter your phrases throughout a document, sit with them, examine how they work together as well read them aloud," she said. "When the right words create the picture, you need everyone to see; the labor-intensive methods pay dividends." Learn to adapt to your priorities. In his attempt to convince someone, Matthew Capala, Alphametic founder and managing director believe that he is adaptable. It is crucial to play on the personality type of the client and understand that their view of the world can affect your thinking. For example, once you go to an expert, it advises that the statistics and details be presented. If the guy is socially inspired, he needs you, so try to establish an emotional connection. "These transactions are not identical," Capala says. "Only one fit-all."

Set the audience up in general.

It is important to talk to others when you want to be persuasive, says John Turner, founder of SeedProd LLC. Your audience is more willing to listen to and buy from you when you make a friendly relationship and build common ground.

"Few people care to listen to and shop from an outsider. You will discover and link to what you have in common," Turner said. "From your own track record, ask questions to help you to find common ground."

While convincing is certainly about your chosen words, it is also about your success story — Nicole Munoz of Nicole Munoz Consulting, Inc. "To blend clear points and solid track histories, you don't need to abandon your path to persuade people, just make the documents weighty for you," she says.

Show your trust and passion.

Sometimes the most convincing argument of all is your own passion and confidence in what you offer or do.

Kasey Kaplan, the founder of KWK Studio, says that "if you can demonstrate your genuine passion because of what you pitch, people can buy in a lot more. "Everybody in an environment with a lot of options, power, excitement, and non-verbal go a long way to persuade people what you sell correctly to them."

5.5 Tips to enhance persuasion skills for women

Although women's business leadership has made significant progress in recent years, we are still facing constant pressure from men and women. It is crucial for us to be as convincing as necessary, whether we are answering concerns from potential clients or asking for wage increases.

A chief can be pushed forward by the force of persuasion. The great news is that women have a great strength of convincing. Yes, a Caliper study found that observed women leaders were more articulate than their males. Here are ten strategies to strengthen women's persuasive tools to improve organizational performance.

1. Take advantage of your strength.

The Caliper study clearly listed the qualities of women's leaders, such as trust, ability to take risks, and compassion. Females can continue to use them in professional environments, where they become important tools, instead of quashing such personality traits.

A woman leader could use her ability to understand, evaluate, and incorporate the feelings of others in such a manner that their listeners' interests are addressed. The female professionals tend to be often milder, which can be much more effective, rather than push everyone to see their perspective.

2. Consider a common ground.

Anyone you encounter will probably share something with you throughout your day. Whether you dislike the continual weather conditions or a shared hobby, such as wine-dining or fine food, this common ground is to be found and used as a springboard. Once you are emotionally linked, people will be more sensitive.

3. Fix an issue

Just ask some questions before you explain your product to anybody. Extract important information to persuade the other individual that your company can help. If you are looking for investment dollars, learn the type of business the shareholder is looking for, then explain how the investor wants your business.

4. Prepare for claims.

More claims will be made against it, the more you're in a specific industry. Over time, a range of approaches to these frequent complaints will be created. The willingness to combat such opposition with persuasive counter-arguments is one of the main methods for persuasion. Before you are in the middle of any of the discussions, make sure that you have trained everyone for all of the complaints.

5. Be constant.

Out of concern that the experts seem too hostile, they also fail to meet anyone daily. Persistence can, however, pay off, especially if there are timing follow-up acts. You may meet a potential customer early in the year for lunch and discover that he is not interested in your company at this moment. Nonetheless, the conditions could alter a few months later. By being strategically diligent, you will find that you may not have made deals otherwise.

6. Do your analysis.

Many people you will meet every day are interested primarily in their lives. The vast majority of the room of a person's business and family. Consider it an activity to study each person you meet in advance so that you can approach them directly. You will most definitely communicate effectively if you go to a meeting and know exactly why someone is involved in what you have to say.

7. Take notes.

Over a single day, workers approach so many individuals that they will be delighted to find somebody who knows them. Ensure your name and important details for each person you meet are remembered. It means maintaining a contact database with the information you have previously discussed, like children's names, current favorite meals, and items. When you see someone at a case, before engaging the individual, you can easily refresh your memory of these small details.

8. Often use names

A person replies to her own name at an unconscious stage. Once you know the name of someone, function it intermittently in the discussion without seeming too obvious. If you realize that some of the world's most convincing people use this technique of ego-building.

9. Mirroring

Studies have found that corporal language is an essential component of discourse and often influences how someone perceives someone else. "Mirroring" is a technique that helps to build relationships. Set your language and actions in subtle ways, as you speak to somebody. Move yours if the weight moves from one step to another. You can adjust the voice volume to suit it to improve the illusion that you work from the same venue.

10. Be fairly confident.

Trust is a significant factor in the success of companies. Many see this as a flaw whenever you project fear. Instead, take the faith that you understand exactly what you're doing in any encounter. Such confidence is infectious.

Today, professionals are challenged to persuade others to accept and understand the way they think. Through building up confidence and using persuasive tactics, female practitioners will monitor any business conference and ability to network, progress, and excel in everything they do.

5.6 Boosting Persuasion Powers

We've all been getting the flood of compelling communications from Facebook ads, fun fliers, interviews, conferences, forums, billboards, and public discourses. We're bombarded daily with thousands of messages that aim to get our attention and encourage us to think, do, and sound.

Today a large range of published opinions on the subject of convincing is becoming a household word in practice. As a small business owner, you might lack a strong tool of control if you did not pay attention to the methods of persuasion that others use.

1. Be smart about the number.

An essay from Scientific America, How Things Cost $19,95, found that it was more effective to use precise figures while pricing products than to use circular estimates. He mentioned a study spanning five years in Florida comparing list prices with both the actual selling prices of homes. The author quoted this study. In the sample, homemakers who reported the homes more clearly— say $494,500 versus $500,000— reached their challenging value reliably. That is to say; consumers were less likely to cooperate with the price down when faced with an exact price.

For example, do not use rounded numbers when pricing your service. This does not mean cheating people but preventing potential customers from reducing your cost below what you are worth.

2. Wear a shirt of Pink color.

In our conscious mind, light is a strong force that can affect our thought, sensing, and acting. Another such hue is Baker-Miller-Pink or, in fact, Drunk Tank Pink or, more specifically, Baker-Miller-Pink.

Drunk Tank Pink: And Other Desperate Forces that shape How We Think, Feel, and Behave is written by Adam Alter, Associate Professor of Marketing and Psychology at the Stern School of Business in New York City. Alter writes in this book about a number of studies in which pink has a compelling effect. Those of us who wore a pink shirt saw donations rise three times, say, door-to-door. Schools that colored their walls pink saw the soothing and engaging students. In fact, research shows the color pink inhibits prisoners' wrathful conduct. As Alter found out last year in a video, our perceptions and aspirations are comforting as we see the shade pink. Perhaps it might be worth trying to wear a rose shirt for a tense negotiating session.

3. Lead the others to Self-Discovery.

Do not tell people why they should improve as you try to persuade people to do anything, for instance, or persuade a hesitant person to alter negative behavior. Help people then learn why they have shifted. "People usually work for their own reasons, not for any other reason," says Micheal V. Pantalon, Doctor of Psychology at the Yale medical school. In the Instant Influence: How to Get Anything to Do–FAST, Pantalon reveals his very efficient influence process based on that principles. The method consists of telling the person who is trying to reassure him to pose six questions:

1. How will you switch from 1 to 10, where one means "not ready at all," and ten means "completely set?" How will you adjust?

2. Why have you not picked a lower number? Or if the person chose a 1, ask them what it takes for this first to become a second.

This second question enables people to express their own motives. If citizens do so, they are more likely to buy in and try harder to stick to the switch.

4. Repeat.

Today's product skepticism is at an all-time high. The "Edelman Trust Barometer 2013" shows that most people have 3 to 5 occasions to receive company information to trust in emails. Please remember that when you want to send a message to convince. Please use different mediums to repeat your message at various intervals. Familiarity appears to increase acceptability.

5. Know what to appeal Principles

Let's say all of you are a financial consultant, and you think your young client was too prudent. You want to convince her to choose more aggressive, more profitable investments in her gender. Tell her what she'll benefit if she opts for more risky investment (including greed), or tell her what she will sacrifice if she doesn't engage in riskier investment (including failure appeals)? Robert Cialdini, Ph.D., a world leader of convincing, suggests that the response is that of calling for defeat. The possibility of losing anything is more enticing to somebody than the possibility of gaining. Cialdini claims that the vocabulary of the failure is inspiring because it is based on the "principle of scarcity." The theory of scarcity is one of the six beliefs of Cialdini. This works on the assumption that we want something less— we are unable to forfeit, but don't want to risk something. This video gives you some detail on all the Cialdini principles.

6. Using baby images

Baby pictures are a strong attention generator–tests indicate our brains are active. They will influence us, too. Let us claim that you are making a report about the avoidance of citrus pesticides. With your message, you can show an orange image. But if a baby substitutes the photo with orange near his mouth, an emotional component can enhance the persuasive power in your text.

Writer Rogers Dolley introduces a significant twist to the concept of using a baby picture to draw attention in Bra influence: 100 strategies to inspire and educate customers through neuromarketing. He also wrote on a review of how people view baby advertising. By using eye-tracking technology, researchers found that audiences focused on the baby's face and paid a little less focus on the news and the commercial. But the advertising logo and copy gained much more exposure when using a side-faced infant picture in which the baby looks to the ad's title. The study found this to refer to any photographs that you promote. The next moment you choose an image in your ad or in your presentation with PowerPoint, it should be remembered.

7. The Motivated System of Monroe.

If you offer and convince your audience to do something, use the guided series of Monroe, a time-tested method, which was the brainchild of Alan H. Monroe of Purdue University. This is the process of five steps:

Step 1: Capture your attention. Crochet your listeners immediately and create them want your message carefully. There are several facets to this: a short story, an impressive numerical argument, a clear quote, a stunning picture, an interview, or a rhetorical question.

Step 2: Create the need. Demonstrate why an issue needs to be dealt with. This is how the audience understands why they should be vigilant. "I have to hear that," or "we have to do something with it!" you want them to say.

Step 3: Set the need. Clarify why a question must be dealt with. That's how the audience understands why they should matter about them. You want them to say, "I have to listen to this," or "We have to do something about it!" Ask your audience how well you can meet this need. This is the answer you need to discuss or tackle.

Step 4: View results. Step 4. Let the listeners see the benefits of your ideas or recommendations through a constructive depiction. Then you imagine them negatively— help them to see the downsides to taking no action.

Step 5: ask for the action. Your aim is to get them to think, "This is a great idea." Describe explicitly what you want to do. The goal is to make people say, "I want to. Tell me how to do this." Learning a few concepts of persuasion and learning strategies for influencing them allows you to communicate more effectively and to improve the company's chances of success. Nevertheless, honesty and dignity must be the fundamental basis for using any convincing tools. So, confidence rules when it relates to persuasion.

Chapter 6: The Human Mind and Mind games

6.1 Human mind

The core of the psychoanalytic theory is the understanding of the human mind. Since the introduction of Sigmund Freud's theories in the early 1900s and following the many developments in the study of Freud's essential thoughts on psychoanalytic theory, the forming of views on the nature of the human mind has maintained a stronghold.

Psychopathologies that lead to mental illness within a subject area at the center of Freud's theory. It is Freud's premise that three levels of awareness or consciousness are contained within the human mind. It is the emergence of these psychopathologies, which affects people and therefore needs more than just thinking about them. Psychoanalysis is the effective treatment of these deep-seated psychopathologies.

Throughout most of human history, the idea that our thoughts must be part of conscious awareness and that the mind is, fundamentally, a domain to which we have immediate introspective access seemed to be an apparent and perhaps even essential reality. In reality, my thoughts seem to me to be clearly understood. After all, it's my stream of consciousness that they pass into.

6.2 What are mind games

Definition: An intimidating or manipulating psychological tactic

Examples: Two main examples of mind games are:

Negging: In order to mitigate his / her social status, you subtly insult a person to encourage seduction of him or her. An example of something a guy might say to a woman from a website: "You know, you look exactly like my little sister. Strange." This is a mind game because it suggests: one, that you're superior to her because you're older; two, that she's not a sexy being to you; three, that there's something strange about even being around her.

Hot and cold: In which you are totally one minute (or day) into a person, and then away from the next, as a way to regulate the relationship. When you do this, you snatch moments of an intimate relationship and, without committing, create false hopes. You also keep the other person off-balance in order to keep you in control of the relationship. There's a lot more. They are techniques of manipulation in general. The couple plays mind games platonically in some kinds of relationships; however, more often, this is done without permission, and so many see it as a form of emotional violence.

In general, when the actions and words of an individual do not match and when they don't align with their expressions of the past. These are mind games.

Mind games lead the target to doubt their judgment, ability to reason, or ability to think. The end result is that they're going to make you rely on the other person to make your choices for you because you can't trust your own ability to make your own best decisions.

Most of us play mind games because it makes us feel secure and stops us from taking responsibility for our emotions. The downside of playing mind games is that you never really have an intimate relationship with people and, therefore, never feel a deeply loving relationship that comes from honesty and trust.

6.3 Some Common Mind games

Seven common mind games are listed below.

1–Disqualifying. This is a way to say something hurtful to someone and then do a double-whammy when they get hurt by making it seem you didn't mean what they thought you meant at all. You can say to somebody, "You're so gullible at times." If the person gets hurt (which you want consciously or unconsciously), you'll answer, "Oh, I was just joking. You are so over-sensitive at times. "Not only do you upset them once, but you hurt them again, disqualifying what you said first and then criticizing them. This can be both angry and confusing for the other person.

2–forgetting. The game is played by passive-aggressive personalities. We basically forget important things like schedules, commitments, debts to be paid back, and the like. You're waiting for them to remember, but they don't, and when you bring it up, they're replying, "Oh, I'm so sorry, I've forgotten." And they say, "God, I'm so sorry. Are you angry? If you're telling them if they're upset at you, they're shouting, "No, God no. If I were, I should say to you. They make you feel mad at nothing that makes you angrier. That's how they're "dumping" their frustration on you without allowing you the opportunity to voice your frustration.

3–Persecuting. Sometimes people project and persecute their hatred onto others. Either they don't know their own hatred, or they think it's justified. They search for reasons to persecute once they start projecting. If the hated people clash on policy with them, refuse an invite, or act the wrong way, the persecutor may find a way to threaten them. We can gossip about them behind their backs, get others to gang up against them, or speak to them in a condescending or disrespectful way. They judge and treat them as bad or evil. They're never talking about their feelings or trying to do things. This is the reverse of the golden rule, "Look to others as you would have them do to you." It might be added, "Punish others for not being what you want them to be."

Guilt-tripping. The game here is to make somebody feel guilty if they don't do what they want to do. A woman calls her husband a sexist, and at first, he may complain, but ultimately, he seeks to be the kind of husband she wishes to be in order not to be a sexist. A husband says she's frigid to his wife because he wants her to feel guilty of not having sex with him. So instead of simply saying to one's spouse, "It makes me feel hurt when you do that and that," which would lead to a discussion that might require both of you to look objectively at yourself, one simply calls the other a name and stirs up guilt while avoiding reality.

5 –Gas Lighting. The term "gas-lighting" comes from Ingrid Bergman's classic film, in which her husband tries to make her think she's going crazy because she's watching things (such as on and off-gas lights). The person says he doesn't see that at all when she sees the lights going on and off. This method is used by some really disturbed people on a disliked family. They're saying and doing stuff and then claiming they've ever asked them. The gas-lighter begins to question the wellbeing of the other as their companion continues in bringing up these things. "I think you may have an over-active imagination, my dear." The disturbed person does not even realize that he or she is doing it at the time.

6–Shaming. People who play this game express their anger when they seek to catch people they don't like to say or do something they think is inappropriate. Idealizing someone is the opposite; it is demonizing someone. A militant religious individual may wait to say the "wrong thing" to those who are not religious. "Religion is not always pleasant," somebody might claim. Then the religious nut might hop on them as if they were a demon, spread their quotation in an offensive voice throughout the internet, and call for apologies. The game allows the shame to spill his or her rage and pose like a good, concerned citizen to the whole planet.

7- pretending. It can take different forms to imagine. To get laid, a man can pretend to be interested in a woman. In order to lead him on, a female will claim to be attracted to a man, thereby acting outrage. People may pretend not to be angry when they are actually in great displeasure. People can profess to be your best friend to make you trust them while hiding their real motives. Good pretenders are good performers. They also convince themselves often that they are serious. They call this a reaction-formation in psychoanalysis. A person may get jealous of you, but they deny it to themselves and convince themselves of the opposite, that they wish you the best. You could fall into their trap if you believe such an individual and regret it. Pretending is a way to control you and prevent any conflict that may occur out of integrity.

These mind games are bad when they take place among adults, but some parents unwittingly play these games with their kids, leaving them hurt and confused. All of these games have benefits, but at the same time preclude true friendships and happiness, which really make life worth living. Stay away from those who are playing these games, moving towards those who are not.

6.4 people who play mind games

They're self-conscious, and they need all the control. Most offenders are quite dull, and they desperately need drama to fuel their being to feel alive and useful. It can be good or bad if someone has all the power to write you back or not. There are many women out there who enjoy and get off to squirm men for their own selfish gain. Do not accept mind games, put an end to them if they arise, or if you choose to invite those negative people into your life. Keep in mind; people are hurting; people are hurting. It seems all people play mind games, and most of us are unable to understand it. Though, I do not sound about individuals like a shark. The games shark-like people play is entirely self-serving, while the rest of us are simply trying to manipulate our realities towards a successful result.

From birth, we were all forced to live up to the tags that those who "loved" us enforced onto us. While our completely well-meaning parent figures shaped and developed us into their understanding of who / what we are, any hopes we had of unique-ness had to be put on hold. Each child ever born is compelled to engage in mind games without a doubt. I don't think the human race knows any other way to survive.

I'm saying that because I think you're referring to mind games that aren't as harmless or well-intentioned, but it's still important to understand that we usually operate on the same assumption, barring an extremely troublesome or horrific childhood. Personally, I've found that most people don't really care to help others succeed. And even those who truly hope for your success do not ignore the emotional pain of other men. I can go as far as to say that you have found your own way of separating yourself from what could otherwise become an emotionally challenging situation. In my view, this is what it all boils down to. We all play one kind of mind game. Without first reaching spiritual enlightenment, no one else can or will ever know the true effect of their words or deeds on another person. To decide what kind of games a person plays, it's just a matter of knowing the signs. Identify what you're not going to accept, analyze why you feel that way, and agree to engage actively. That's how to surmount it. Best of all, for you.

6.5 How to avoid people playing mind games?

Of course, manipulative individuals should be discouraged in general, but they're around everywhere, we're just deceptive, more or less, and you can't avoid the whole universe. Speak about this topic with other people; we all understand this; they will advise you what to do in certain cases. You should identify what manipulative people exactly do, how and why, you must become very attentive. Beware of everything, their actions, their voice and words, their body language, etc. Read a lot of books on this topic. You also have to think a lot. No one can tell you exactly what to do in any case, always. When you identify your mistake and their manipulation, think to get solutions, do researches. Begin to correct yourself and be very diligent. Observe what others (successfully) do to deal with people who are manipulating. You're going to build so many mistakes, but you're going to get better over time.

Identify the weak spots and defend yourself. You may be too generous, and you may not be able to say no, and people are using you. Perhaps you are emotional and vulnerable, and you are weak to nice words someone says to you to manipulate you. We are all foolish in some way. Be suspicious of everybody, whatever things are serious or ordinary! (Especially if it's money) You've got to do with someone, do research first, get ready. Take care of your expressions, don't speak too much, avoid talking about personal things.

This depends on which groups of people. Some enjoy each other's mind games, others like to dish it out but can't take it, others just loathe the whole practice. For the latter type, I would say the best first response is to speed up one's process of recognition, i.e., recognizing a) that a game of mind was actually started and b) the target of the game if possible. So, you make the decision. Would you like to spar at this level? Is that going to put you in danger? Answers to these questions no / yes mean avoiding them.

If you can't avoid it, like in a workplace situation, you will also need to identify the game's object. Though you can't base your judgment on how you thought, because sometimes people who are always searching for a goal for their games are very successful at what they are doing, and sometimes you shot yourself in your foot (in which case you need to be stronger at it than you are). If you need to play, watch as much as you can while remaining as non-committed as you can. Does the perpetrator have an end in sight, or is it a simplistic mind game aimed at you because they are bored? Anyway, stand in contact with your land, log all, be consistent in interaction, be the one that stops every discussion, and don't smile. The aim is to stop it, not to perpetuate it — ideally the champion for you.

Only the individuals who really love the thrill of mind games will hope to find each other and keep their emotional stilettos far away from us. Although watching from the bleachers can be an interesting game. People play mind games for a number of reasons, but the aim is typically to gain a sense of influence or dominance over someone else. The player wants a specific response, but instead of telling you what they need or pressing for what they want, by using manipulative tactics, they try to meet their desires. It's all about feeling strong and in command, but those emotions never last a long time. This usually doesn't end well whenever we want to use someone else to make us feel better. If honest communication is absent from the photo, creating a meaningful bond with someone is almost difficult.

The best thing once you know that someone plays with you is to bless them with affection, to stop speaking, and to move on. Manipulators have poor personal boundaries and are not interested in your best interests. They also established destructive strategies of coping and are unlikely to change. It can be difficult at times to tell the difference between someone from a person who is intentionally trying to manipulate you, who might be a little insecure or socially awkward. Check here for some things to help you work it out.

You feel like being judged or compared with others.

A common game of mind is to make you think you're not measuring up. You could hear things like, "My last wife never had a late issue with me" or "No one else seems to care about it. This action is the adult version of peer pressure and is designed to make you do something you don't want to do or feel a certain way about yourself. If this is done to you by the person you are dating, it is not about you. The real problem is their fear and the need to make you feel less than you are. For them, you are a mirror, and the way they speak to you is the way they speak to them in their inner self-talk. Don't buy your criticism from them.

Your version of events or a discussion is often claimed to be false, and it makes you question your wellbeing.

Maybe the most insidious mind games are called "gas-lighting." Someone who uses this deceptive technique may say something, then deny that they've ever said it, or convince someone that their gut feelings are all in their heads. We want you to doubt the reality in order to feel out of control. I had done this to me lately, and I felt I was losing my mind. When you feel like you have to justify yourself or backtrack constantly, you're likely experiencing this extremely harmful form of psychological violence.

The person with whom you are dating seems to be really inside you, and then for days, even weeks disappear.

For a number of reasons, people do not call or answer messages. We get busy at times; we lose interest at times. Nonetheless, there are some people who deliberately avoid talking in order to get your attention. They do this to manipulate the relationship, or as a check to see what the response is. Tons of books are all about "playing hard to get" as a good way to keep a person engaged, but it's pretty dishonest. If someone is playing this game, the best way to find out is to ask them if they are. Let them know how you feel, see what they're thinking about. Explain why you want more contact from the people you date and a direct approach. If the behavior continues, it shows a lack of respect for you; and if you cut them loose, it could be for the best. It will only lead to a toxic relationship to get involved with someone who views you in this way.

Chapter 7: Hypnotism a mind hacking process

An unusual altered state of consciousness characterized by certain distinct signs, the most conspicuous and invariable of which is the appearance on the electroencephalograph of persistent alpha waves, extreme suggestibility in the subject, the focus of attention on a single stimulus, and a sense of "oneness" with the stimulus. Different techniques applied to oneself or another cause hypnotic states.

The hypnotic condition may or may occur spontaneously in a large percentage of normal individuals. It is recognized as having an association with normal sleep, as well as with a number of trance-like states, including somnambulism, coma, and Hindu yogis and fakirs' trances, as well as numerous tribal shamans. In fact, hypnosis has been known in almost all countries and periods of history in one form or another. Originally known as supernatural research, hypnotism has achieved a definite medical reputation, even only in recent years, and no mean position in legal medicine. Nevertheless, the tradition is inextricably interwoven with ritual activity, and even today, most hypnotic manifestations are connected with the supernatural and mystic, so that a knowledge of hypnotism remains a necessary component in any sophisticated comprehension of our own period and past magical world science.

7.1 Hypnosis and control of the mind

Hypnosis is not a "mind control" game as it is not a form of manipulation. The typical "man on the street" associates' hypnosis with mental control, as this is how hypnosis is often portrayed in films. No wonder so many people were terrified of being hypnotized! The initiation of hypnosis itself is a joint effort in collaboration between the hypnotist/coach and the subject/volunteer.

This looks during a stage hypnosis demonstration as if the hypnotist entertainer has the power to do almost anything for the hypnotized participants.

Obviously, this interpretation of the audience actually contributes to the performance's entertainment value and helps hypnosis seem even more enigmatic. Hypnotized volunteers ' experience on stage is actually more like a comfortable daydreaming state. They feel good, and within those parameters, they have offered to encounter experiences in hypnosis. What are the boundaries? The Stage Hypnotist offers a brief pre-talk about the myths and misconceptions about hypnosis before calling for volunteers. The pre-talk establishes the program's limits. The introductory statements of the Stage Hypnotist build an "implied contract" about what will happen to the participants during the demonstration of hypnosis.

Usually, the implication is that some bizarre and unusual hypnotic phenomena will be experienced by volunteers, but no ethical or moral lines will be crossed. If the Stage Hypnotist breached a volunteer's implied contract, they would usually pop out of the trance state feeling like, "Hey, I didn't sign up for THIS?!"They might choose to step off the stage right away.

7.2 Hypnosis and Brainwashing

People often mistake brainwashing with hypnosis, but they are not connected. Often, the hypnotic experience comes from a free-will participant interacting with a mentor to achieve their goals (i.e., losing weight, feeling experiences of coma, etc.). On the other side, brainwashing is the product of suppressing the free will of an individual and restricting their ability to make choices to the extent that true "fact" cannot be discerned. Specific techniques of brainwashing could use confinement, deprivation of sleep, torture, and drugs. Through coercive physical and mental manipulation, brainwashing, and mind-altering substances, these programs seem to focus on mind control. While these may be the focus of clandestine government programs, this is not the stuff of the hypnosis world of today!

You're very open to whatever the suggestions in a hypnotic state. If a hypnotist asks you to consume strawberry ice cream, you can "taste" it and "sense" a cool feeling in your throat when you drink simply because much of your conscious mind is bypassed by thinking, assessing, and deciding. In the traditional sense, you're not really "thinking," but you're "experiencing" without questioning. It can be associated with the sense of absorption in an exciting book or movie when you are very ignorant of the world around you. You may lack inhibitions when you are hypnotized and do recommended stuff that you would otherwise find mortifying, such as a public birdie song performance. Yet your sense of justice and survival is deeply entrenched in your amygdala, so you're not going to do anything reckless like trying to fly out of the 10th-floor window, thinking you're an eagle. You're not going to do something you don't really want to do. Your free will remains intact, and your conduct is not compromised. The power over life, your mind, and your body are with you. Such an event may sever the bond between a concept, recollection, or perception and the stress and pressure which surrounds it. It can help change what needs to be modified and build what needs to be developed.

Suggestions and other hypnotic effects, psychological techniques, imagery, and vocabulary constructs are created and used in hypnosis mind control, so you can accomplish something you want or gain from, and in this hypnotic state, tolerance reaches much further than in non-hypnotic states.

7.3 Effects of Hypnosis

An important factor here is that the ability of people to think logically and objectively declines in a trance. We tend to accept clearly any information given to them, without considering whether or not it is rational and reasonable. This means people are suggestible in a hypnotic trance; they accept any suggestions given to them uncritically. This means that even people who are strongly eager can be hypnotized and made to do things they would not normally do. It suspends rational analysis, conscious decision-making, and independent judgment. This is a blessing to members of the group who, after all, don't want to think about themselves! You have a strong set of tools to influence people, even forcing them to do actions that contradict their own morals and ethics.

What the manipulators say...

Interestingly, many leaders of cults will often claim that people cannot be made to do things against their will, even using hypnosis of mind control. Two things that are critical here are

1st of all, group members are expected to embrace whatever the leader says. So, they're going to tend to support this notion. Second, implicit in the idea is that if the person does something, they willingly do it; it is their own decision to do it. When we make our own decisions, we believe more firmly and are more committed to the outcome, and our decisions ' actions and effects last longer. It's a very quiet but strong notion.

Myth about hypnosis

One thing to remember is that hypnosis is not always a system of a closed eye. To be in a trance, you don't need to have your eyes closed. Have you ever traveled anywhere, for example, and you don't recall much of the trip until you reach your destination? You've been in a dream! During dream conditions, people frequently drive when their eyes are fully open and functioning! If you see someone stopping in front of you, there's no trouble braking yourself and doing what's needed to prevent collisions. People often have the idea that to induce trance, there are special hypnotic words. In normal-sounding conversations, hypnosis can be induced by using everyday words without saying' relax," deeper' or' sleep.'

Important points

Some key points to remember are:

- hypnosis is essentially an altered state

- we actually experience plenty of altered states or trances ourselves every day

- it is not mandatory to have your eyes closed

- hypnosis can be triggered without speech, and most critically

- it decreases cognitive skills and the ability to evaluate data.

7.4 Theory of Hypnotic action

Among numerous explanations of the physiological conditions that accompany the hypnotic state, there is one, the theory of cerebral dissociation, which has been generally accepted by science and can be described as follows briefly. The brain consists of countless groups of nerve cells, all of which are more or less closely connected to each other through nervous links or variable resistance pathways. When sufficiently strong, the enthusiasm of any of these classes, whether through experiences obtained through the sense organs or through the transmitted behavior of other groups, may give rise to an idea's consciousness.

The resistance of the association-paths of the nervous system is relatively low in the normal waking environment, so the behavior is readily transmitted from one neuronal unit to another. Thus, the key concept which enters the upper stratum of awareness is attended by a flood of other unconscious ideas that has the purpose of testing the primary idea and avoiding its complete dominance. Now the unusual superiority of one single system of ideas, indicated by the practitioner, along with the total elimination of all competing schemes, is the main fact to understand in hypnosis. To some extent, the conditioning hypnosis of the physiological process suggests an analogy with normal sleep. There is a reduction in cognitive anticipation and a proportionate rise in the resistance of neuronal connections as one composes itself to sleep. This is obviously what occurs through hypnosis, the subject's basic passivity elevating the association-paths ' resistance. But in normal sleep, unless there is some thrilling reason, all neurological structures are at rest, whereas in the hypnotic state such a total suspension of cortical operation is not permitted, as the operator holds alive the collection of sensations relating to himself by speech, movements, and manipulations of the patient's limbs. Therefore, a neural system is segregated, so that any concept proposed by the operator is free to work out itself in practice, without being exposed to the tests of other ideas ' sub-activity. Depending on the degree of hypnotism, the alienation is less or more complete, but a relatively small increase in resistance in the neural links is sufficient to secure the dominance of the hypnotizer's suggested ideas.

Hyperesthesia, so frequently mentioned in conjunction with the hypnotic state, always belongs to the questionable category, because it has not yet been determined whether or not there is a true sharpening or refinement of the senses. Furthermore, it may be argued that the correct interpretation of poor sensory experiences, which tends to provide proof for hyperesthesia, merely reclassifies the idea that the anticipation transmitted by the sensory nerve acts with exceptional intensity, being released from the constraint of sub-excitation in neighboring neuronal groups and structures. By bringing forward this point of view, it must be accepted that inadequate sensory sensations will work on the nerve and brain in the conscious, aroused state, just as they do in hypnosis. Nevertheless, they are so stifled in the former case in the middle of a plethora of identical experiences that they fail to reach an awareness. In any event, the subject's sometimes unusual resistance to minor sensory stimuli is as accepted as anesthesia itself, a reality of hypnotism. If not entirely justified, the word "hyperesthesia" may be extended to the observed phenomenon for the sake of a better term. A second person does not automatically trigger the hypnotic condition. "Spontaneous" hypnotization and "self-hypnotization" is well established. Many yogis, fakirs, and shamans may create a condition in itself that closely approximates hypnosis by sustained eye fixation and other methods. The mediumistic coma is also a case in point, as will be shown below.

7.5 Hypnotism and Spiritualism

The later spiritual thinkers and even earlier astrologers and magi promoted the interaction between ghosts and what is today called hypnotism. It has been shown that manifestations of a distinctly hypnotic nature are related by a certain proportion of the witnesses to the working of spirit entities, whether angelic or supernatural. So Greatrakes and Gassner claimed that they had a supernatural power to heal diseases. Witchcraft is believed to derive from the witches ' trade with the devil and his followers, in which the power of hypnotic suggestion seemed to have worked to a large degree. Cases of hysteria, catalepsy, and other coma phases are granted a spiritual meaning, i.e., spirits, gods, elementals, etc. are supposed to speak through the possessor's mouth. Even in some instances, such intelligence is associated with the bodies of dead men and women, but usually not until Swedenborg. Although the Modern Spiritualism movement dates accurately from 1848, the year of the Rochester rapping's, the origins lead directly to the animal magnetisms. In addition, Swedenborg, whose affinities with the magnetics have already been mentioned, had a remarkable influence on America's and Europe's spiritualist thinking and was also a precursor of that faith. Even then, unconscious manifestations were a characteristic of magnetic coma, and clear-sightedness, supernaturalism, and telepathy were generally believed in and thought by many to be signs of divine contact. In Germany, among those who retained views on these lines was Professor Jung-Stilling, C. Römer, Dr. Werner, and poet and physicist Justinus Kerner, who conducted his studies with a somnambule that became popular as Prevorst's Seeress— Frederica Hauffe. Hauffe appeared to be able to see and converse with the deceased's spirits, and she gave evidence of prophetic vision and insight. In her presence, physical phenomena have been witnessed, knocking, rattling chains, moving objects without contact, and, in short, manifestations characteristic of a poltergeist. Furthermore, she was the originator of a language "primeval," that she proclaimed to be the language spoken by patriarchs. While Hauffe was only a somnambulist or magnetic person, he later had all the attributes identified with active spiritualist mediums. There were also many situations in England connected with mesmerism of a paranormal nature. Dr. Elliotson, one of the best-known English magnetists, was converted in time to a theory of spiritualism as an explanation of the clairvoyance and similar phenomena that he thought he had observed in his patients.

Nevertheless, France, headquarters of the rationalist magnetism school, had much less of a spiritualist view to give. However, the latter theory also existed in that world at intervals before 1848. J. A competent physicist and a severe character in magnetism, P. F. Deleuze, who wrote his Histoire Critique du Magnétisme Animal in 1813, was said to have accepted the teachings of spiritualism until he died. However, it was Louis-Alphonse Cahagnet, a man of humble origin who started to study somnambulism about the year 1845 and experimented with somnambules, who became one of the first distinguished French spiritualists. So fine was the evidence given by Cahagnet and his subjects of spirit interaction that it remains among the movement's most outstanding. In the United States, it was first prompted by the research of magnetism by La Roy Sunderland, Andrew Jackson Davis, and others who were founders of spiritualism. Hypnotism and understanding of the role of spirits associated with each other until 1848, when a definitive separation takes place, is seen elsewhere, and the two go their separate ways. The split, though, is not entirely complete. Second, the mediumistic trance is clearly a form of accidental or self-induced hypnotism, while in the second, many of the session room's more startling manifestations have been consistently replicated in animal magnetism reports. Of instance, in the cures of Valentine Greatrakes or Mesmer and his followers, the diagnosis of illness and prescribing of medicines prescribed by the command to the "healing medium" have their model. Automatic phenomena— speaking in tongues and so on— formed a signature aspect of the trance triggered and associated conditions early on. Even some of the subsequent physical phenomena connected with spiritualism, non-contact activity, rapports, and rapping's were encountered in association with magnetism well before the phenomenon identified as modern spiritualism was recognized. It is viable to trace the process of hypnotic suggestion in the unconscious phenomenon, just as in many of the physical manifestations, we might detect the product of deception.

7.6 Hypnotism and psychical phenomena

Hypnotism and cognitive symptoms Psychologist Paul Joire identified the three typical stages of hypnotism in the 1890s:'

Lethargy, the condition of total exhaustion with varying levels of anesthesia, with neuro-muscular excitation as its central trait. In this phase, the participant has eyes closed and is usually only marginally open to suggestion.' There is full anesthesia, and there is no sign of intelligence. This condition is defined by immobility. **"Somnambulism**, the position of the face differs; the person tends to be asleep. A brief touch or stroking along any limb is sufficient to make the leg stiff. Suggestive is the main characteristic of this disorder. Somnambulism poses three degrees: awakening somnambulism, mild passivity with a reduced will, and decreased suggestively.

Chapter 8: Relationship between Hypnotism and Persuasion

Despite popular belief, self-hypnosis is all hypnosis. Each hypnotization is self-hypnosis! That is to say, with the advice of a professional hypnotist, the subject hypnotizes himself, and the participant may at any time agree to accept or reject the proposals. Therefore, you or anyone else can't control hypnosis. There are, however, hypnosis methods and theories that can be used in the company and in personal partnerships to provide better communication and convincing.

The values, self-image, and self-worth are the strength and usefulness of hypnosis. As Patrick Wanis ' hypnosis reveals, once you believe something is a reality, it is possible for you. It's normal. He had hypnotized the participants in the shows of Patrick Wanis and said that they had recently experienced the funniest thing on earth and couldn't help laughing, and the more they look at Patrick, the more they laugh. Such people laugh intensely, and some people even joke until they sob. They're smiling. How can we do that? You thought you saw the funniest thing on earth.

Patrick Wanis invites an audience member to go to the stage of business environments and literally show their power of confidence. Patrick tells the professional to raise his hand parallel to the ground and to stiffen his neck while Patrick Wanis forces it back. He is now telling the woman to close her eyes and say ten times (with passion and convictions), "I'm soft." Again, Patrick is again lifting his hand. The crowd and volunteer disbelieved and were surprised because of the apparent faintness of their arm, and the volunteer could not hold it straight. The same volunteer is now being called by Patrick to exercise the same way, and this time ten times (with emotion and conviction) repeat, "I'm strong." Look, she and the public are just as much shocked as the arm is now strong and firm.

Obviously, what occurred was that the body of the volunteer addressed her words and feelings and her self-confidence.

What do you think of yourself? Will you believe in love, peace, wellbeing, happiness, and prosperity at the most profound level you deserve most in your life? What do you suppose you can accomplish? Will your convictions empower you to be happy, or will they keep you low, weaken you, and rob you of your happiness?

Did you know what your body always questions your convictions? The stage hypnosis show probably provides the best illustration of mind over body energy. I'm hypnotizing people and saying, "You're on a deserted planet now. You have nothing to drink for two weeks. It's very warm and dry.

"You're thirsty and warm. You are going to open your eyes in a moment, and you are going to be 10x thirstier than already, and that you will come to me. You're going to take three big bites. You're going to chew it gently to quench the appetite. "When it's over, you will go back to your place, close your eyes, and fall asleep." It is immediately obvious, upon raising the eyes, that these men are hypnotic and hungry. You see them panting heavily and moaning for water, loosening their collars. We come near me and occasionally even drive each other away from the way to the pike in my side. Three big treats were taken and gradually chewed. The sense of happiness and satisfaction from eating the fish is on all levels. We head back to their seats happily and fall asleep. Clearly, their appetite was calmed down.

Now you think, what's so special? The audience laughs at me, and at the same moment, they are in total shock because they see that what such hypnotized people just ate was not really a fresh, healthy, juicy cod, but a raw oignon. I'm only getting through to the group. Hey, an unpretentious onion! So, what did happen? Why did they eat and not feel a raw onion? Why haven't they spit out or frowned at the horrific taste? Why wasn't one even crying? And how could they chew so long and not flinch so slowly, but rather seem to like they really liked it? You were so profoundly hypnotized that the onion was not seen, felt, or eaten. Our minds convinced our bodies that what they consumed as a meal. We won't get hurt, if somebody is allergic to onions, because the body doesn't know the onion-it assumes that it is a peach.

Another truly incredible aspect is here. Twenty or 30 minutes later, when the show ends, I approach my hypnotic themes and say that their breath stinks like onions. When they come out of a trance, I say. Although they don't recall chewing an onion, the fad flavor suddenly takes over, tearing up in their eyes often. Now, this is the mind's strength in motion! Through everyday life, the same logic applies to us. What do you think you should accomplish? Would you agree that you can be tall, happy, and healthy and warrant that? Would you believe your feelings can be regulated or managed? Would you think you have the energy and potential to be content at any given moment and choose happiness? Would you think you've got the ability to blow up? Clearly, your confidence isn't just the force of your will; it's also a good idea. If you can (with emotion) visualize yourself to be and do something, it is real. This is partially the cycle of shaping and modifying values. All we see and hear. It is valid for us that we embrace such issues.

8.1 The four-minute mile of Roger Bannister

The first four-minute mile in recorded history was run by Roger Bannister on 6 May 1954. England's 25-year-old born ended in Oxford at 3:59.4. He said in an initial straightaway, "It is the potential to get more of yourself than you have." Roger is talking to the power of faith once asked to explain the first four minutes and to the practice of record-breaking. Since the success of Roger Bannister, thousands of people have completed the four-minute miles. What is the reason? What is it like? Now thousands of people will sprint at the same moment as they figured they should. You may recall, 15 years ago, airlines used to hold brown paper bags on each passenger's seat because so many people were vomiting on flights. Such bags no longer make sense, and a person vomiting on a plane is almost unheard of unless he is ill or intoxicated. Why does it happen? What has changed? Our riding views have shifted. For most of us, the second nature is to fly on an airplane. We've had no more the same opposition and uncertainty we've had before. It has changed our beliefs.

8.2 The theory is reasoning and satisfaction

Patrick Wanis claims that our ability to detect our weaknesses and strengths and then forget, try to love ourselves and others is key to activating our capacity. Instead, we adjust our view of ourselves and our trust in what we deserve and what we merit.

The more you value, the more things you want. The more self-esteem you receive, the more people you get along with. When you evolve, those around you react differently to you. If you feel confident, secure, and in love with yourself, they can make you feel good around you. It is one of the key things to persuade.

The second key is that you enter the world of another person to perceive and hear as you see (see the world and enjoy it from your eyes). Then, you should lead them comfortably and respectfully with the correct methods and tactics to the result you seek. Such experience and knowledge can be used for personal and business, administration, corporate management, and marketing relations.

Throughout Patrick's view, acceptance and the release of negative feelings, which in turn allows us to appreciate this time, freely express ourselves without anxiety, to understand our dreams and goals, and to express love and success, are the key to happiness.

Hypnosis is often described as a method, but in reality, there is a huge difference. Hypnosis is a mental state. The formation of an idea is a suggestion. The two fit together well, as hypnosis enhances the suggestivity of most individuals, rendering them more responsive to feedback than they would in "natural" levels of consciousness. In the hypnotic state, we use ideas, and indeed we use solutions to establish hypnotic environments or transformations, as some people know. The traditional way of doing this–a music hall reference today, even if some people still use it –is the phrase: "You sound like you're sleeve-e-p-y-y," repeated over and over. While it might seem scientifically insane, it does indeed create a condition of hypnosis if done properly–but it is not often very effective. Instead, when the person is actually under hypnosis, we give recommendations for things to happen: "I want you now... r-e-l-a-x... deeper and deeper..." And we're also using something which seems much more obscure to the uninformed–a post-hypnotic suggestion. Here, we suggest to the listener that after the session has been over, she will think or feel, or perform a certain task, and will safely return to the "normal" state of consciousness.

8.3 Suggestion is all around us

Suggestion is not only used within the system of hypnosis. It's like: "From this day on, you will always be more and more comfortable." You will see illustration everywhere:' Queueue here' is a famous one–that's a clear recommendation. They all need the advice, and you will see instances. "10,000 volts" is another suggestion, but indirect. In fact, it says: "Keep away, or you may die! "Some of them are extremely subtle. Go to the waiting room of a doctor or surgeon to find people in benches. What are you doing? Well, of course, you are also sitting down. Nobody had to explain to you that you wait your turn–that's just what you do. Experience and prior learning and teaching come into all we do. You are expected to slow down or to accelerated as you approach if a traffic light is stuck in orange. You don't beat your eyelid if you are asked if you give your assistant a £ 5 bill for a thing costing £ 3.10: "Have you got the ten bills? "And yet more than the cost of the item you have delivered. It means, of course, that you are going to receive £ 2. Yet, this time, it is just an implicit comment. This implies, however, two things–one, that you get £ 2, and two, that the store assistant will change slowly. "Can I take your coat, and what about? "When you reach a dining room? You presume that perhaps the individual is linked to the service and transfers your clothes to a stranger. You actually don't even bother watching it. In far more than one movie where the mask is stripped off the door and in a waiting car, this specific situation has been used for good comic effect. It's amusing due to the ridiculousness of the scenario–yet the circumstance is only awkward if we know what it meant. Voice tones, environment, dress style, daytime, age, apparent class status, self-exposure, these and many other things come into play here. I think this suggestion may be accepted, simply because it is so scandalous that we cannot think it would be made if it were not. I think it is worth mentioning here. So, it works a trickster of confidence. Offer a hint in a plausible way that in some respects, something seems to be natural, and some kinds of people may fall for it. That's how people have very often tampered with money–typically with somebody who wants to be some form of royalty or a director or other contractor, who is ready to share his / her most recent wealth since it needs an instant cash boost. That's how girls are at times charmed by the unexpected partners and how people are sometimes convinced to send huge sums of money to a lady they don't care about. Sometimes the idea deals with envy or vanity, sometimes with psychological vulnerability, sometimes with pleasure. Almost always is ridiculous, irrespective of the heart.

One of the main things to examine about such a fascinating subject is that in order to ensure the acceptance of a suggestion it should be either simply not firstly observed as a suggestion simply as a statement of fact, but also completely required by the person receiving it. Suggestion works when something is actually wanted to be done. Whether for hypnotherapy or daily life, the person must really want to accept it, like what is offered, and seek. How convenient is it for you to sell a car you're still hunting for? You can't waver because of the price before he tells you just one thing you didn't think about or didn't understand. You want to do that. Naturally, that's why you sit in front of your salesman first and foremost. The choice of purchasing but not buying is your call. Instead, he informs you of the great news–this car has just been updated, but you can obtain it at the old price. This product does have a reservation, but if you agree that you want it today, it's yours, it actually a special order which the customer didn't want, but you can afford it at the cost of the standard model. Perhaps this will not be a special edition, or it has an engine larger than standard, or it has a longer guarantee. What the dealer wants depends on what you're going to respond, but it's all advice. The argument, of course, is that you have to purchase this car right before someone else does. You have to justify that proposal, so it bites because you like to buy the vehicle. Regrettably, marketing a car is much simpler than forcing an ego to accept change. That's what we mean by' full of hearts '–if any' healing' is to last, the inner self must want change too. Nevertheless, in mind, there is opposition, so in the first position, there is a question. We need to offer a different, though more beneficial attitude to the unconscious of mitigating this. We'll have someone like this who's too scared to move. This is most likely because they are afraid of losing power and falling–so that the effect of self-protection persists. Hypnotic advice may be used to reflect on how quickly the person has trust in the driver, the vehicle's full response, the joy of the facilities with that he or she switches position, and so on. The transition can be impressive when these thoughts are processed in an unconscious manner. The value of well-formed hypnosis recommendations There is many examples of using the advice in hypnosis. Nonetheless, five extremely important criteria are expected to be adhered to in order to create high-class recommendations that actually work. Positive sentences Avoiding uncertainty Intensity generate curiosity Provide no active complaint. Let's take a brief glance at each. This is the following expression. They can stop, where possible, pessimistic phrasing; terms like, can't, shouldn't, couldn't, or wouldn't, would not. Negative phrasing Negative things can be used, but those must be done conceptually, as shown by "You won't have to smoke cigarettes..." in which' no need' is a fact. Avoiding confusion, it's soft and fluffy as you place the head on the pillow. This is an enigmatic statement–is it a smooth, fuzzy head and pillow? Of reality, we know what is meant precisely, however actually the unconscious functions so we must ask what we mean exactly! We discussed this topic in-depth now, but to summarize. A strength of interest Every idea that we make for hypnosis would obviously not be successful if it doesn't trigger a strong interest in the audience anyway. It has to say whatever the individual really wants to do. When we propose anything against the desires of a citizen, the idea is probably rejected. It is even more likely that we do not bypass the aware critical faculty. We also guarantee that our ideas are correct and that nothing is appropriate to the audience. The existence of feeling is necessary for hypnotic ideas to be considered. Dr. Hippolyte Bernheim suggested this notion in the late 1800s for the first time. He said that the existence of emotion is effective in helping hypnotic suggestions, and while emotions can be positive or negative, the emotion of joy can also be produced by making amazing suggestions that an individual wants to hear.

Chapter 9: Persuasion in different aspects of life

Persuasion and influence are important skills for achieving personal goals in all walks of life and are commonly found in everyday life, especially in school, work, or even in the family as a persuader and convincing. It is indispensable to lead a fruitful life to be able to exert personal influence to change the thoughts and behaviors of peers and other people and to defend oneself against theirs.

9.1 The basic mnemonic

The efficacy and knowledge of persuasion are equally important in this complicated world. It's one of the vital life skills to impart abilities, and riveting human relationships prosper when you learn basic persuasion skills and communication skills while presenting. In addition to win-win goals, an admiring persuader should have a strong speech with a simple, concise, and positive tone, a robust marketing structure that is transparent and up-to-date, an appropriate body style that fits the delivery, and good stage use. All these characteristics and behaviors are fundamental elements of persuasion expertise in communication.

This basic mnemonic, TABLETS helps you memorize the fundamental elements of persuasive presentation with examples:

1. Thoughts / Attitude

2. Articulation/Pronunciation and language

3. Body-language / Nonverbal communication

4. Logos or Logical

5. Energy/Enthusiasm

6. Topic and Content

7. Stage Presence

9.2 Throughout Persuasion, thoughts and actions display Emotional Intelligence: Ethos of Persuasion

While improving emotional intelligence, even a mediocre facilitator can be effective in providing an admiring message.

Or put it simply, emotional intelligence is about 4S: self-awareness: persuaders are conscious of their abilities (intrapersonal behavior) self-management: persuaders can strive or control their attitude. (Intrapersonal abilities-subliminal capacity to persuade) Social awareness: persuaders who are informed of their audience. Social management (interpersonal attitude): persuading people to learn how to manage their community. (Interpersonal skills) This encompasses all the soft skills and social skills, such as courtesy and professionalism you display to your group, personal competence, flexibility, personal values, imaginative problem-solving skills when coping with audience questions, successful communication, including compassion, constructive responses to audience requests, ability to say "No" as participants turn away from audience questions.

Articulation

It is very necessary for a facilitator to pronounce words accurately with specific stress. If you're not sure how to pronounce certain terms, search online dictionaries as some of the top online dictionaries, including Merriam and Oxford, have audio captured for almost all English words and their variability.

Definitions of few frequently mispronounced terms such as climate, state, query, recommendation, and representative can be found in online dictionaries that explain principles of grammar for both American and British.

Body Language is a Visual Persuasion Tool

Examples of a professional body language include good eye contact, good posture, good hand motions, and a facilitator's formal actions. Always make sure that you do not use postures and movements like shaking arms, scratching head, shrugging shoulders, and narrowing eye-brows as these actions will draw the audience's attention from the main idea.

Language

Words with structure and quality will complement the language. In addition to good grammar and material management, vocabulary usage plays a vital role in a speech. Registered facilitators use a variety of communication resources, including expression statistics, rhetorical devices, literary devices, and stereotypes. Similis and metaphors are a few basic vocabulary numbers, although procatalepsis, humor, onomatopoeia, zeugma, and pun are few sophisticated examples of linguistic instruments widely used in a speech.

They are also good at using verbal communication tools such as report building statements, compliments, speech transition statements, assertive communication, and negotiating skills. Therefore, speech should be stripped from interference in the mother tongue, linguistic fillers, judgmental phrases, repetitive terms, derogatory comments, and generalizations.

9.3 Energy, Enthusiasm, Entice, encourage are Pathos of Persuasion

Once you learn the prosody of voice, you will put all of the above Es. Until convincing, you should, of course, be excited and motivated if you "strongly agree" with the points below.

Will I enjoy the subject I will be presenting?

Do I have a strong belief in the topic I will be presenting?

One can perform icebreaker games and energizers to bring life to the performance in order to bring energy and enthusiasm. And beginning the presentation with strong activation and attention-grabbing comments are some directions throughout the presentation to maintain the enthusiasm.

Topic and Content is the King

Topic

Make sure you are content with topics and subtopics that are not only interesting but also engaging. Ideally, which subject and subtopic will address the basic questions of 5 Ws and 2 Hs that include Who, What, Why, When, Where and How long and combine jokes, roleplays, icebreakers and energizers.

Content

Your content may be subdivided into IBC mnemonic (Introduction, including self-introduction, careful grabbers, body, and conclusion) so that the audience is clear about what you want to say.

Stage Presence

A Professional Persuasion Technique Such inquiries must be answered while the stage is being used. Am I standing in a position where everyone can see me?

Am I seated on both sides of the room in the right direction?

Am I avoiding some prominent distracting on-stage movements like tennis court movement, chained elephant movement, or pendulum movement?

Should I keep a good gap from the audience?

Now, before persuasion, enrich the TABLETS and inspire the crowd as never before. The mnemonic is helpful for recalling some of the core elements of convincing to produce a successful speech effectively.

9.4 How to convince others through persuasion by using leverage

Leverage ensures you're learning how to maximize yourself and get a lot more out of the hours you're putting in instead of doing it all yourself. Through the efforts of others, you leverage yourself by getting other people to work with you and for you to achieve your goals. Sometimes you can ask them to help you on a voluntary basis, although without any personal reward, people won't work for very long. You can also hire them to help you at other times, thus freeing you up to work with a higher value.

The management concept is "Getting things done through others." You need to develop your personal power and learn how to convince and manipulate people to work in a shared direction in order to be a leader. Therefore, both outstanding administrators are also great salespeople of low pressure. Alternatively, they don't force people to do things, they persuade people to accept those tasks, with clear timelines, and they decide to quality standards. When an individual becomes persuaded that he has a vested interest in doing a job right, he acknowledges the job's control and the outcome. Once a person accepts ownership and responsibility, the manager can confidently step aside, knowing that the work will take place on schedule.

You should understand how to persuade others and grow your personal power by always knowing that there are only two ways to accomplish the things you want in life, you can do it all by yourself, or you can do most of it by others. Your ability to communicate, persuade, negotiate, influence, delegate, and effectively interact with other people will enable you to develop leverage through the efforts of others, knowledge of others, and money of others. Developing your personal power would empower you to become one of the organization's most powerful and influential people. It will open doors for you in any area of your life by knowing how to convince and influence people.

9.5 Persuasion in business

If you're in business you're in worldwide business Whether you're employed in a large corporation with a footprint in all major markets, or you're a sole website owner-operator, your messages are likely to reach individuals from a wide range of cultural backgrounds. Such social factors make it even more complicated and difficult to consider customer decision-making and actions. Persuasion is not only for marketing purposes. Each business leader persuades employees to work in compliance with organizational principles and policies. Every business leader is persuading suppliers to provide great service at good prices and supporting companies. Many top managers spend more time trying to impress others than planning policy. So, let's get persuasion stronger.

Whether we are a consultant, a freelancer, an entry-level worker, a C-Suite manager, for our clients and us, the job we do has to push something forward. Sometimes this means getting the people who work with us and the people who sign our paychecks to follow our suggestions on what to do. It's a question of persuasion if you want to get people to do what you want. Whether you want to push a huge organization or get someone to fund a small event or venture that you are organizing, persuasion is the secret to positive action. Persuasion is a technique that calls for such measures. Know the audience Persuading someone you've never met and understood nothing about is challenging. Understand what they are going and what they are thinking with. Get inside their wants, expectations, and wishes.

Ask for their short-term goals and reaffirm what you learn while listening. When people tell you what they are trying to accomplish, explain your interpretation by restating in your own terms what they are doing. So, if I understand you correctly, which means you want to describe situations that could do what they aim and make happen. Ask for future obstacles to their ambitions. Let them continue to talk until you fully understand what they are experiencing and really want to help them get where they want to go. Learn how to make choices regarding their operation. Figure out who has to be "sold" to adopt a new concept.

Say that by aligning their ambitions with your own, you will support them. In the light of how it will help them, offer the concept, idea, or strategy. Please point to the target and potential obstacles you described and demonstrate how your advice can eliminate the obstacles and push them towards their objective. Explain how they are working with your plan, project, or idea. Reflect on the positives of their case, not what you admire, but what makes sense. Champion the benefits with all the passion that drew you from the beginning to the idea or project.

Build a strategy for introducing them to the larger group. Ask how quickly you and the colleagues and payroll signers can be convinced to take part. Step back and let the cycle belong to them as you talk. Those who handle a corporate culture well are those who realize that persuasion works better than argument. It's important to stand up for your morals and support your experience, but the introduction can be better than the whole conversation.

9.6 Persuasion in media

The mass media is a part of the mass communication process. There is no denying that the media are the main features of generating people's thoughts for one culture. But to understand the effect, it must be emphasized that there are different possibilities of impact depending on the subject. It should also be considered the rule that the less the consumer's primary experiences (speaking of young people or people who have tasted their lives very well) or the capacity of the information, the greater the capacity of the media's influence. The more it is reported for an event, issue, or occurrence, the more the public opinion is provoked, and the interest of a higher rank is maintained. Media control can be loosely described as' direct or indirect effect on cultures or, best said, rough or subtle public opinion exploitation.' Politics and the media's shared impact is very growing. The informational role of the means of mass communication can be seen to a large extent in their mutually conditioned partnership. Under the circumstances of today, a huge degree of political truth in one society depends on the kind of impression the audience gets from the media's political events. As a result of the public opinion's interest in politics, the media are focused on political factors and events. The media and politics ' shared involvement is mostly seen in the media's mutual feature. However, apart from this, the press still carries out other roles of their job, the most important of which are the theoretical, investigative and strategic function (as well as the Press Watchdog feature).

As part of the usual activity and tradition of the journalist, the media not only relay the signals and knowledge from the political factors but also evaluate, select interpret, express their opinions and represent their own attitudes towards them. We often question and express views and perceptions of other knowledgeable people and associations (professional persons, ex-doers of public functions and responsibilities) while speaking about arbitration, various gaps in their working and desires are often shown in the news activity.

The media's basic goal is to allow the public to know what's going on in the world. Media serve people in this way, while at the same time receiving income and profits in the sense of increasing reputation and trust in regard to the objectivity of the data they reflect. Here is also the privilege of the public word's regulations.

Getting influence is closely linked to the benefit that the media can make. The media is interdisciplinary areas that discuss subjects that are above all important and pleasing to the percipients, and the first position in politics. That's why the media sells information that they can take advantage of. Public debates and public political issues that are being held on our Television are a topic of interest to the majority of the population, which is why the lady is a marketing company from which the press knows their biggest benefit.

In films or entertainment events, the most lavish ads are not shown, but after or during political content programs where the participants are high government officials addressing important and vital social issues. Most media advertisements are directed at persuading the audience to believe or do something. News stories use several techniques to make viewers believe the story is factual, such as direct quotations from known sources.

Through marketing, social affairs, and lobbying, the media communications often associated with persuading us will be identified. Commercial advertising is trying to persuade us to purchase a product or service. Public relations (PR) "sell" us good business, policy, or institutional picture. Politicians and advocacy groups (groups supporting a particular ideology, point of view, agenda, or action) try to persuade us to vote for or help them by using advertising, statements, surveys, blogs, and other methods.

Such "persuaders" use a variety of techniques to catch our interest, to build legitimacy and confidence, to activate the demand for the item or strategy, and to encourage us to behave (buy, vote, give money, etc.) We call such tactics the "language of persuasion." They're not new; Aristotle wrote more than 2000 years ago regarding persuasion techniques, and they've been used by speakers, authors, and others.

Advertising

Advertising is the simplest starting point: the bulk of advertisements are relatively simple in nature, easily available, and in their original format. Beginners in media literacy were motivated by studying advertisements to learn the language of convincing. Keep in mind that multiple media messages, such as TV commercials, often use several strategies. Some use one or two randomly.

Political Rhetoric

When used by leaders, government officials, lobbyists, or advocates, political rhetoric is more difficult to analyze, not only because it includes more emotional issues, but also because it is most likely to be seen in bits and pieces, sometimes interpreted or condensed by others. It is important to identify the methods of argument in public discourse because the implications of that discussion are so important–war and peace, fairness and inequality, democracy and exploitation, and the future of our planet.

The media today have a complex relationship with the sources of power and the political system of democratic societies. Firstly, they should provide facts and opinions free from state and power interests; second, they will encourage news and information directly related to political parties and other organizations. Nevertheless, the connection between mass communication and the result of politics has always been similar. The good informative role is very clear in the partnership between politics and the media. Communication content, as part of news practice, not only passes signals and data from political factors, but it also analyzes, picks discusses, provides its own viewpoint, and expresses opinions towards them. Media effects on elections are understood by deceptive and propagandistic persuasion methods, contrary to the professional standards and requirements for mass media communication functioning

Social media persuasion

Social media's role in generating and maintaining public opinion is important. The position of free and independent media in the democratization cycle is much greater because it leads to development and freedom of expression and thinking. "Within modern societies, obtaining information is vital to the performance of decision-making between people and policymakers. At the same time, the interaction itself is transformed with the rise of the mass media and its capacity to transmit information and feedback from entire populations. With a larger scope for electronic media, coupled with the greater influence of journalism and marketers, the media has turned into a more basic social body, changing the existing civil society organizations as a central way of linking people with the broader social and political system. The media has been observed for a longer period of time as protecting citizens from the government's misuse of power. "The media has been a source of citizenship for a longer period of time, known as a fourth power, a power that opposes government decisions that could have had a harmful effect on the people.

The media is the only one that has the greatest impact on our perceptions, opinions, and desires. It is the media with its combination of languages, image, tone, and context that is the main source of information in the twenty-first century and has a tremendous influence on the public, creating a society's values.

9.7 Persuasion in health

Communications in public health often try to persuade their audience to adopt a particular belief or pursue a specific course of action. Public health professionals tend to accept the ethical defensibility of reasoning to a large extent; however, a couple of experimental studies challenged the ethical defensibility of convincing risk and safety interaction. Nevertheless, the common use of rhetorical techniques for discourse on public health requires a close look into their legal status, regardless of previous critiques.

Persuasion is a process that is influential and can appear in many different forms and situations.

In the field of social psychology, persuasion is characterized as an appeal to change a given object's attitude or assessment (Petty & Briñol, 2008). Since the response is outlining the reasons and role of the petition, the communication can be the most influential factor in changing attitudes. In the above situation, the food industry places great emphasis on product names because the meaning extracted from the names will convince a person to look beyond an objectively unfavorable food concoction and instead view it as an undeniably friendly item.

When convincing messaging will persuade people to prefer harmful things, so persuasive messages should also be able to coax people into healthier behavior and attitudes.

As it is, there is a significant and growing relationship between persuasion and the field of health communication. Public messaging included campaigns from "Only Say No to Drugs" in the 1980s and today's "Let's Change" movement to identify and alter specific behaviors and make people safer. When shown by these cases, psychological persuasion is associated with improving the emotional aspect of behaviors in particular to persuasion in the health field. This is because there are certain health problems that have dire consequences, such as diabetes, but can be resolved by relatively simple behavioral changes such as dietary changes. The delivery of such medical advice and data can be particularly powerful in influencing the responses of individuals to these behavioral changes and the health issue itself.

Consequently, a great deal of psychological research has studied that persuasive factors are most active in health messaging While a significant amount of research has been dedicated to persuasion as applied to the health sense, the wording and verb attitude involved in the delivery of messages along with the intervention goal in the message content need review.

9.8 Everyday persuasion

Persuasion is almost everywhere. I tried to count the number of direct attempts; I encountered in a single day to control my thoughts and behaviors. This included people asking me to do something, pushing me to do something, asking me to buy things, advising me to pay for things, reminding me where to stay and when to go, giving me messages to repeat, songs to recall, behaviors to change, and beliefs to embrace. I skipped the radio and newspaper in the morning because I realized that I couldn't count that quickly. I lost count somewhere around 500 before I left my office in the middle of the week.

We exist in a complex world of attempts to influence. A large part of the population makes a living simply by getting others to fulfill their demands. Conservative estimates say that within a single day, an individual can obtain up to 400 convincing appeals from advertisers alone whether a director who promotes efficiency, a cop who controls traffic, a dealer who opens a deal, or a dictator who advises us that we need to spend more money on social programs— every one of us is exposed to countless attempts at manipulation every day

Let's just focus on the mass media, a major contender for your attention, time, and your inevitable compliance, most profitable. When you watch the normal amount of tv, you'll see 100 television ads every day.

If your task was just to do the average amount of mass media viewing, listening, and learning, you'd be there 8 hours a day, seven days a week, 375 days a year! (No, that's not a misprint— you couldn't get it completed at this rate in a year. You'd have to work overtime.) And that doesn't even include the hours you've spent interfacing with working people. For example, it has been reported that general managers invest more than 80% of their time in verbal communication— mostly attempting to cajole or reassure fellow employees. Don't ignore your family, your parents, your friends, acquaintances, and many others you encounter over the span of an ordinary day— all of whom want you to do something and seek to get you to do it. My point of view is that a culture is a large group of people controlling, persuading, questioning, requesting, cajoling, exhorting, inveigling, and otherwise exploiting each other to progress their lives.

We consider it society because instead of being overtly intimidating, we persuade Think if every effort at persuasion is substituted with coercion— the owner of the store whacking you across the knees because you didn't buy the jacket, the supervisor kicking you in the belly to make you work faster, the cop just firing you down for 45 mph in a 35 mph zone. You would be a physical wreck after the typical day. On the other side, persuasion makes society work smoothly— while physical coercion is preventing it. Successful persuasion makes physical intimidation, interpersonally, and globally, needless. Society thus profits from persuasion.

And those who know how to persuade are most benefited by society.

10. Conclusion

Persuasion is the act of persuading people to change their beliefs or to do something that you advocate. People have often defined persuasion as a delicate form of art, but what exactly makes it so powerful? Understanding the art of persuasion can not only help you learn how to influence others; it can also make you more aware of the techniques that others may use to try and change your beliefs and behaviors. Persuasion is not a form of art in the same sense as painting or music but involves the finely tuned creative skills-or language and communication art. Persuasion, though, requires some of the characteristics of more conventional forms of art. It is intellectually challenging, nuanced, articulate, and completely true to your persona. You may question why you should bother learning how to persuade someone. You may even think that such an "art" is diabolical or manipulative. The fact, though, is that at one time or another, that successful person was in a place where they had to convince somebody of something. For example, many people have to persuade an employer to recruit them before they can even start working and earn money. Salespeople are persuading people to buy goods or services. Politicians are persuading people to support them and vote for them. Con artists convince people to fall for the schemes they don't have and spend money. You may convince your instructor to take a makeup exam, encourage your girlfriend or boyfriend to get engaged or persuade someone to assist with your volunteer program. In general, finding people doing anything without some sort of persuasion is pretty hard. Like any other art form, persuasion is in and of itself neither optimistic nor neutral. It is how you use the art of persuasion, and for what reason, which decides whether you are making a meaningful contribution to the world.

The failure to persuade others in life can be a huge handicap. You may find it difficult to get a job, buy a home, or take the next step in your marriage. On the other side, you can notice that for every scheme posed to you, you are too easily convinced and dropping. If so, there are several ways to reduce the vulnerability to dropping for each slick, which exists. A therapist can help you improve your self-esteem, develop social skills, and even learn how to manage anxiety. Such factors make you less prone to disappointment. Persuasion is not just for a salesperson. You're constantly influencing others. You may be influencing your children to do their homework or an employee to spend their work on Saturday. If you can be successful at influencing people, you can get more done, and life is easier. Those with strong skills have a smoother path through life. Persuasion skills can be extended in all, friendships at school, at home, and even to encounters with outsiders. Apparently, some people are born with the ability to lead and influence others. The art of persuasion is knowledge of communication techniques, which, through reminding others of your point of view, will help you achieve your goals. Detecting, particularly from someone who is fluent in it, can also be challenging. With the strategies and instructions above, you'll be well on the path to becoming a persuasive master-and one that's safe from being exploited by other masters.

11. References

Art of persuasion: 20 skills. (n.d.). Retrieved from Lifehack: https://www.lifehack.org/

Everyday persuasion. (n.d.). Retrieved from Working psychology: http://www.workingpsychology.com/index.html

How to influence others through persuasion. (n.d.). Retrieved from Braintracy.com: https://www.briantracy.com/

Hypnosis mind control. (n.d.). Retrieved from ControlMind: http://controlmind.info/index.php

Hypnotism. (n.d.). Retrieved from Encyclopedia.com: https://www.encyclopedia.com/

Ogami, K. (n.d.). Persuasion in the Health Field: Framing the Message of Attitude Change. Persuasion in the health field.

Persuasion in Everyday Life. (n.d.). Retrieved from Paperblog: https://en.paperblog.com/

persuasion skills. (n.d.). Retrieved from Management study guide: https://www.managementstudyguide.com/

Types of persuasion. (n.d.). Retrieved from Literary Devices: https://literarydevices.net/

What is the persuasion. (n.d.). Retrieved from Betterhelp: https://www.betterhelp.com/

www.ingramcontent.com/pod-product-compliance
Lightning Source LLC
Chambersburg PA
CBHW051223250726
48655CB00006B/2564